THE MUSE IN COUNCIL

THE MUSE IN COUNCIL

BEING ESSAYS ON POETS AND POETRY

BY

JOHN DRINKWATER, M.A.

DOCTOR IN THE UNIVERSITY OF ATHENS

BOSTON AND NEW YORK

HOUGHTON MIFFLIN COMPANY

The Riverside Press Cambridge

1925

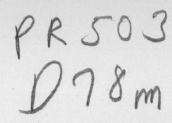

The Riverside Press
CAMBRIDGE · MASSACHUSETTS
PRINTED IN THE U.S.A.

TO
FERRIS GREENSLET
GOOD PUBLISHER, GOOD FISHERMAN
AND
GOOD FRIEND

10150

NOTE

THESE essays, relating to the theory of poetry and the practice of several poets, were written at various times covering a period of fifteen years. I do not claim that the opinions expressed are consistent at all points, nor should I wish them to be so. Although we may be constant in our love of poetry, our moods and reasoned views about so wayward a divinity cannot but know their changes too. But in collecting these papers together for the present volume, and looking them over for revision, I find, as I should have hoped, that there is at least a general attitude towards poetry governing them all, and that appreciation has been subject to that attitude always. Every reader will quarrel with conclusions here and there, but my anxiety is not for agreement, but to leave such readers as will treat this book as a whole with some clear impression of what I conceive poetry to be and what its function among us. These studies have been written, as the old title-pages have it, on several occasions, and no one of them affects to be exhaustive in itself. But, with how much deliberation I cannot tell, they have taken shape as chapters supplementing one another in a single design, and as such I would ask for their consideration.

1924.   J. D.

CONTENTS

CONTENTS

THE MUSE IN COUNCIL

. .

THEORIES

There is a feeling that it is dangerous to examine too nicely into the way poetry works . . . I think, on the contrary, that the closer you look into poetry, the more you have to discover, and to enjoy.

LASCELLES ABERCROMBIE

THE MUSE IN COUNCIL
.   .

THE POET AND COMMUNICATION [1]

THE immediate trouble about all æsthetic theories is that when they are first propounded nobody understands them. By far the most interesting critics of poetry have always been the poets themselves, although it may be said, in passing, that some poets are quite extraordinarily bad critics. But it is strange to find how often a poet, who is at his own creative work all lucidity, can become in his theory full of difficulty. It is beside the point to say that anybody interested in poetry can understand clearly enough the creeds professed by Dryden and Wordsworth and Shelley and Matthew Arnold. Certainly we can understand these to-day, but then we have been learning how to do so for anything from two hundred down to sixty years; we are apt to forget that when we read a book two hundred years old we are profiting in our understanding of it by all the understanding that has been brought to it by the generations before us. It is when we come to the critical theory of our contemporaries that the difficulty is manifest. There have

[1] *Conway Memorial Lecture.* 1923.

lately been published an unusually large number
of books dealing with poetic theory. Some of these
have been merely superficial journalism, written
without any wide knowledge of English poetry or
its history, and showing no natural gifts of judgment. But there have been others which are real
contributions to the subject, and are likely in time
to take a place with the considerable poetry itself
of this age. But I cannot believe that any honest
reader can pretend that these books are easy to
understand. I have lately read, for example, Mr.
Lascelles Abercrombie's essay 'Towards a Theory
of Art,' Mr. Robert Graves's 'On English Poetry,'
and Dr. Strachan's 'The Soul of Modern Poetry.'
All three are responsible, well-informed, and acute
work. It is doubtful whether the metaphysical
nature of poetry has ever been so subtly stated before in English as it is by Mr. Abercrombie; a
patient reading of the work will, I think, convince
any competent reader that this is not an extravagant claim. Mr. Graves's essay is a much more
mercurial affair, just, as it were, the personal notes
made by a poet in-between-whiles upon the processes of his own art. It is more often than not un-
convincing, but it was not written to convince, and
it remains a very charming record full of independence and personality. Just as Mr. Abercrombie's
work is important as a contribution towards the
metaphysics of poetry, so Dr. Strachan's book has

real originality as a study of the moral philosophy of poetry. And yet though I know all these books to be admirable, there is a great deal in each of them that I cannot understand at all. Dr. Strachan is relatively plain sailing, although even he often persuades us in his gentle way to take things on faith instead of showing any good reason why we should do so, but Mr. Graves says things at times that seem to qualify for a place in Mr. Lear's 'Book of Nonsense,' where the joke always is not that something silly is being said, but that something is being said that isn't anything, while Mr. Abercrombie, although he never comes within a thousand miles of saying anything that is nonsense, says a great many things that leave me painfully aware that I am but a very poor simpleton. But the fun of the whole thing is, if I may by way of illustration be personal for a moment, that I, who never say anything that is not as plain as the turnpike, am told by Mr. Abercrombie that I have precisely the same effect upon him. Nobody I know will accuse me of presuming to place myself in Mr. Abercrombie's company either as a poet or critic, but we are old friends and that is how we affect one another in these matters. The whole truth of the thing is that critical theory is nearly always less intelligible than the art with which it is dealing, because, while the essential condition of art is that completeness of form which makes the thing created easy to perceive, critical theory is always incomplete, full of loose ends, and largely dependent upon the definition of terms about which no two people in the world are in agreement. In the course of time any particular poetic theory of great distinction is sanctioned by a common consent as to what it means. We may disagree with Wordsworth's view, for example, but we to-day do know what that view really was, or at least we all of us agree that we know this. But in Wordsworth's own time even informed opinion was not sure what he meant. It is not even vital that the interpretation which we make to-day of Wordsworth's theory may conceivably be one from which Wordsworth himself would dissent — a fact which we are apt to overlook. The important thing is that we have made out of his statement a very significant piece of poetic theory as to the nature of which, though not necessarily as to the importance of which, we are now of one mind. It may be suggested that the same thing happens about poetry itself, but I do not think this is so. It is perfectly true that any great poem, 'Paradise Lost' let us say, has a more obvious significance to us now than it could have had to its readers when it was published. That is to say, we approach it now with all the assurance bred of two hundred and fifty years of habit, and our minds, because of our ancestry, are able much more readily to perceive the full beauty of the poem. But this perception of beauty is a different thing from the understanding of a meaning, and while it is easier for the new reader of 'Paradise Lost' to appreciate its grandeur as poetry than it was for the original reader, it is no easier for him to understand its meaning, and he has to apply himself with as much individual intelligence to that task as was necessary in the beginning. But with poetic theory the case is different, it might almost be said that it is reversed. An instructed reader, coming across Matthew Arnold's 'Preface' in 1853, must have known at once that here was somebody speaking with the voice of authority, but he might very well have been excused for not exactly understanding what the voice was saying. We to-day can only confirm the first impression as to the authority, but we can very much more clearly catch the purport and implication of what was being said. In short, it is the profounder quality in any work that most profits by the revealing processes of time. In 'Paradise Lost' the doctrine is of less fundamental importance than the poetry, and it is the poetry that has grown in dominion with the passing years; in the famous 'Preface' the art was little and the doctrine much, and it is the doctrine which has gained in definition.

Much, therefore, that we may perhaps now find difficult in such a book as Mr. Abercrombie's will no doubt be very easy going to readers two generations hence. But he raises one question with his conclusions about which I find myself in positive disagreement at once. It so happens that Dr. Strachan, by an independent process, confirms Mr. Abercrombie's opinion, and since the matter is one which must very profoundly affect any theory of art, and particularly from the artists' own point of view, I should at least like to try to state the other side of the question. My admiration for the two books in question I have already recorded, and anything I may have to say is said with a due sense of obligation. Mr. Abercrombie, then, in his essay 'Towards a Theory of Art,' writes:

Several theorists having assumed, as they must, that art is expression, go on to point out that expression is not communication, and conclude from that that communication is a mere accident in art, as though the artist in his work were just talking to himself, and we happen along and overhear what he is saying. This is mere confusion. . . . What happens when an artist makes a work of art? He makes his experience communicable: and in order to make it exactly and perfectly so he will spend the whole force of his spirit. . . . If æsthetic experience is the condition of art's activity, the essence of its activity is communication.

This passage is, I am aware, in a very elaborate context, but I do not think that Mr. Abercrombie would consider it unfair to set it apart. The argument seems to me to be fallacious in this respect, that while we may agree that art is expression, I cannot conceive of any clear thinker about the matter holding that expression is not communication. Mr. Abercrombie says that there are such theorists, but I have not come across them; indeed he allows that even they are forced to admit that expression is communication, though by accident only. The whole point of the matter is to decide what is communication. Communication to whom? If it necessarily means communication from the artists to other people, then I do not at all believe that communication is in any important way the 'essence of art's activity.' If it may be put so, I believe that the real cause of art is the necessity in the artist for communication with himself. Mr. Abercrombie goes on to instance a man looking at a landscape and finding it beautiful. He says that he is not thereby creating a work of art, but that in perceiving the beauty he is expressing his experience 'by the mere fact of [its] being distinctively and decisively known.' He then adds:

Now suppose this man is an artist. He desires, therefore, to achieve expression of experience. But if it is expression in the strictly limited sense, he has got it; he need do nothing more. Yet we know that he will show himself specifically to be an artist by the precise fact that he will do something more. He does not begin to be an artist until he begins to publish his experience. The expression he desires to achieve is external expression. You may say he is merely recording his experience. But for whose inspection? For his own? Certainly: but only

for his own? Ask any artist, if you can charm him into
a moment of candour. Or ask yourself, what are picture
exhibitions for, what are publishing firms for, what are
concerts for?

The answer to this seems to me to be that in merely
looking at the landscape and finding it beautiful
the man quite decidedly is not expressing his experience. He is not even expressing it silently to
himself. He may enjoy it, he may even be content
not to go beyond looking at it. But suppose him
to be an artist, as Mr. Abercrombie says, what
does that mean? It means that in beholding this
thing, a landscape or whatever it is, he feels the
urgent necessity not only of looking at it but in as
complete a way as possible of understanding it.
That is really the fundamental hunger of the
human heart, to understand its own experience,
and it is a hunger that can be satisfied in one way,
and one way only, the taking of parts of that experience, as it were, isolating them from their irrelevant environment, and endowing them with
the concrete form of art. It is precisely this that
this man of whom we are speaking does, and it is in
the actual doing of it that the experience becomes
complete. It is only when he is forced to the extremely difficult business of achieving that concrete
form of which I have spoken that he really perceives the object of his contemplation, that the
experience, in fact, becomes complete. We can il-

lustrate this fact by almost any well-known passage from poetry. We can imagine Shakespeare walking along a Stratford lane in winter, looking at the leafless trees, and thinking of the summer that had gone. But as he did this the experience both of the thing seen and the thing suggested, of the visible object and of the idea, was vague, enveloped in a mist of a thousand other thoughts that had no relation in particular to these things, inducing, no doubt, a wistfully pleasant mood, but not the exaltation of clean-cut imaginative fulfilment. It was only afterwards, when the moment returned to him, and insisted upon itself, and forced him to deal with it with more than the half indolence in which it had first passed, that he braced himself to the effort of putting down in set words 'Bare ruined choirs where late the sweet birds sang,' and the experience became complete. I do not believe that when he was creating that line Shakespeare either consciously or sub-consciously had any desire to communicate his experience to somebody else. I believe that his only purpose was to satisfy the demand of his own mind for the understanding of its experience, or, to keep more closely to our line of argument, to make an imperfect experience perfect. When Dr. Strachan says,

All art means that we have something to communicate. No poet dare claim that he is independent of his audience; otherwise his action in writing, printing, publishing is a sheer contradiction,

he, as it seems to me, overlooks this essential condition of creative process, just as Mr. Abercrombie
does. Of the concerts and publishers, of which both
of them speak, I shall have something to say in a
moment. In the meantime, at the risk of repetition, I want to make my point a little more ex-
haustively if I can.

As to why there should be this hunger in the
human mind, and as to the end to which it is lead-
ing us, I do not know that anybody can offer any
sort of explanation. All we know is that the desire
for completeness in experience, for mastering our
own experience instead of being mastered by it,
is one that dominates our lives. Complete understanding of our experience is the most satisfying
condition to which we can attain, just as total inability to make this welter of experience intelligible to ourselves results in madness. We get examples of this in all sorts of apparently quite
trivial things in the daily affairs of life. We know
how troubled the mind can become when, say, we
are talking to a friend about something quite important, and we are moving logically step by step
towards a clearly seen end in our argument, and
we are suddenly held up by, perhaps, our failure to
recollect the name of somebody who is not important to the matter under consideration and of
whom our friend has never heard. A tiny fragment of our experience, in this case so insignificant

a fragment as the knowledge of a friend's name, has suddenly gone out of control and at once becomes an irritant quality. We know with what an apparently disproportionate sense of relief we may an hour later suddenly recall the name and break in upon the conversation to announce the fact. This is a trifling instance, but, I think, suggestive. The artist is the man who has this hunger for mastery over his experience, for understanding his own experience, more actively, perhaps, than is common. It is at once the glory and the tragedy of the artist's life. The glory because he more than others, is given a way in which to satisfy his hunger. The tragedy because he more than others, again, is desperately aware of great volumes of experience that he can never completely understand. And I believe that in the bringing of this chaos of experience into something like a cosmos in his own mind the artist, strictly speaking, has no ulterior purpose whatever. When he is creating he is not thinking of what his audience is going to say about his work when it is done. If he is thinking about this his work will inevitably suffer, because so surely as an artist begins to think about what people are going to say of his finished work, or, indeed, is consciously aware that they are going to pass any judgment upon it at all, so surely will he, little by little, begin to put into his work something that he thinks people would like to have there, instead of setting down the truth solely for its own sake as he sees it in the light of his own vision. Every artist is beset by this danger, and none, I think, escapes from it quite unharmed; but the law is plain.

While, however, we recognize that this is an essential condition of all worthy creation, that the act of creation is carried through first and foremost to bring completion of experience to the artist's own mind, and that if it were not for this purpose there would be no such thing as art, this is not the end of the matter. It must be understood that the argument implies that the poet, apart altogether from the consideration of an audience, would still actually write his poem upon paper, or at least shape it into exact form in set words in his mind, and not be content with a merely vague emotional perception that took on no concrete form. This same audience does, nevertheless, come into the scheme of art, and in two ways. First, from the point of view of the artist, the position seems to me to be this. Once he has done his work, as loyally as he can, abiding by that first essential condition of art, he has finished with his creative obligations, and becomes a member of society battling for his livelihood like the rest, and hungry, like the rest, for approval and acceptance. With a very human eagerness, therefore, he quite rightly begins to think of publishers, and concert rooms, and exhibitions, and he, quite legitimately, may take a keen interest, even a commercial interest, in the career of the work that he has created. Just as I believe that no honest artist thinks about his audience when he is working, so do I believe that no artist who is also a rational being is indifferent to the public estimation of his work when it is finished. While communication to the world beyond does not seem to be a necessity to the poet in his work, publication of his work to other people becomes a very practical and human desire once it is completed. But, beyond this, communication or publication of his work to other people is of profound importance to the other people themselves, and it is a fortunate economy in the scheme of things that makes him want to hand his work on when it is done. For while the general view of what the use of art is to the world often seems to be wrong, there is no doubt that a world in which the artists created their work without publishing it would be the poorer by one of its most healing influences.

The nature of the influence would seem to be this. The hunger of each mind for the understanding of its own experience is one towards the satisfaction of which nothing is more helpful than communion with other minds that have in some measure solved this problem satisfactorily for themselves. And it is just such communion which is made every time we come into vivid contact with a work of art. Before a work of art, we are in the presence of a mind that has in some measure mastered its own experience, and we come away from the presence with our own mind braced towards the understanding of its own experience in turn. That is the secret of the power of art in the world. It is not that the poets can solve our own problems and answer our own questions for us. My problems are my problems, they exist only in terms of my personality, and it is mere spiritual idleness for me to go to Shakespeare or Wordsworth or Browning, saying, 'Here is my problem, what is the solution; here is my question, what is the answer?' They cannot tell me, nor can any one but myself. But what I can do is to go to the great poets and under the influence of their faculty for achieving lucidity out of their darkness quicken my own powers of achieving lucidity for myself. This means that to value poetry for its message or the nature of its philosophic content is to misunderstand its very nature. If we truly care for poetry and know the virtue to be found in it, we shall profit equally from Wordsworth, who tells us that 'Our birth is but a sleep and a forgetting,' and from Swinburne, who tells us that 'life is a watch or a vision between a sleep and a sleep,' and Browning, who holds that 'We fall to rise, are baffled to fight better, sleep to wake.' Here we have three poets coming to three vastly different conclusions upon much the same speculation, but that does not matter. The point is that each in turn has been able to see his own philosophical experience so clearly that he has been able to reduce it to this excellent clarity of form, and it is that shaping faculty which stimulates our faculty to its own rich purpose in turn.

To hear people talk about art is generally to get but a very misleading impression as to what its real effect upon them is. This is, perhaps, most noticeably so in the case of the theatre, the most democratic of the arts. If we leave out of the question the great number of plays that make no abiding impression at all upon anybody and consider only those to which the spectator does return in his mind some days after he has seen them, we find that people even here rarely talk about the thing as intelligently as they feel it. A man will watch a fine play in the theatre, and respond to it with fulness of emotion, and delight in the subtle intellectual structure and movement, and talk irrelevant nonsense about it at lunch the next day. He will almost certainly find himself arguing about the argument of the play; instead of recalling the manner in which the argument has been presented, praising that for its excellence and censuring where it fails. That is the true business of criticism, and one which critics, both amateur and professional, very commonly forget. For one person who can deal justly by the imperfections of a work of art, which is to do something of great spiritual significance, a hundred can chatter volubly about the artist's conclusions, which really do not matter to anybody but to the artist himself. If we rejoice in the presence of a vivid work of art, we should be able to carry that spirit of enjoyment with us into the world, braced by the strong imaginative life of which we have partaken, and it is no more than an impertinence for us to think it important to other people that they should know whether we do or do not happen to agree with the moral or psychological argument of that life. We have every right to complain if the life is not real, real, that is, in the sense that it was something about which the artist himself was convinced at creation, but we have no right to complain that it is a life of which we are not able personally to approve in our sympathies. Translated into terms of abstract life, we doubtless do not like Malvolio, but under the touch of Shakespeare's art we should be just as happy in his presence as in that of Viola, who is all grace. But the world is seldom good at reducing its emotion to reason, particularly when that reason has to come out at the end of a pen. I have known many critics enjoy a performance in a theatre, for example, quite simply in their emotions, who have yet reported nothing of that enjoyment when they have written of the event afterwards. In their actual experience most people are sound in their relation towards art, but in the defining of that experience they habitually come to grief. In reasoning about art they persist in applying standards not of imaginative virtue but of doctrine, and they blame the artist not for defective vision but for what he sees, so that still Pope is justified —

'A fool might once himself alone expose,
Now one in verse makes many more in prose. . . .'

Of the sufficiency for the artist of this communication to himself we are, perhaps, most tellingly persuaded when we are sometimes with forgotten and uncelebrated work. I was lately reading the love elegies of an obscure eighteenth-century poet, James Hammond, whom Samuel Johnson included in his 'Lives' only to dismiss as negligible, and who has since come to no better luck than a contemptuous reference in Mr. I. A. Williams's recent 'Byways Round Helicon.' Hammond, by his work as a whole, has deserved better treatment, having more art and feeling than Johnson allowed, and having a mood of tenderness not very common in his generation. It is true, however, that, for the most part, the fervour of his love escapes us in his verses, in which there is often an expectancy of the perfect word and no realization. Then, suddenly, in one poem we come across this stanza,

'With thee I hop'd to waste the pleasing Day,
Till in thy Arms an Age of Joy was past,
Then old with Love insensibly decay,
And on thy Bosom gently Breath my last. . . .'

With the exception of the one phrase, the stanza is no better than its fellows, but with his 'old with Love' Hammond stumbles upon revelation, and for one moment is a poet with the best of them. There was some very vivid brightening of the emotion when he achieved that, and I do not believe that in the orderings of Providence he captured the phrase chiefly so that he might communicate that brightening to some lucky reader two hundred years later. I think that Providence wanted just once to be kind to the poet Hammond himself, and gave him that phrase in token of the good-will. I do not suppose that since he died Hammond has averaged one reader a year, but I do not think that to himself the significance of his moment was any the less for that.

The modern school of painting that refuses to represent anything that can be related to a natural image is inspired by this determination that its art shall be judged as art and not as doctrine. This does not mean at all that in the literary arts doctrine should have no place. The poet may bristle with convictions and be all the better poet for it, but it is not seemly in us to praise or dispraise him because of the nature of these. How does he present them, how does he stimulate us in the shaping of his vision, how does he quicken our faculties in the exercise of his? These are the questions, and these alone, by which he comes up for our judgment. That he is human and treasures our good opinion of his work when it is done, even of the kind of man that his work embodies, is a circumstance of which it is dishonourable in us to take advantage. When his work is finished he may be hurt or gratified by opinions passed upon these false premises, but at the time of creation he knows better than this and would despise us for them. In the long run the only good-will that he truly cherishes is that which comes from an audience which makes nothing of consent or otherwise to his doctrine, but acknowledges in him that abundance of life which is alone the negation of evil. There is no deliberation in the lovely service which the poet does to mankind. It is his to

> '. . . bless
> The world with benefits unknowingly;
> As does the nightingale, upperched high,
> And cloister'd among cool and bunched leaves —
> She sings but to her love, nor e'er conceives
> How tiptoe Night holds back her dark-grey hood.' [1]

---

[1] My friend, Ernest de Sélincourt, has drawn my attention to the fitness of these lines from Keats to my argument.

THE POET AND TRADITION [1]

EVERY poet spends his life between the devil of imitation and the deep sea of revolt. So far as his deliberation controls his working at all — and it may be said that deliberation is an energy in the creative mind as vital as the more mercurial habit which we call inspiration, that it is, indeed, the patient conditioning of the moods from which inspiration springs — it is concerned more than anything else with the sorting of individual experience with tradition. Given creative energy, it is upon just dealing in this matter that all hope of its happy employment depends. For just as the idle surrender to tradition, the mere pilfering of another man's constructive achievement, is the most ignoble process of the mind, so the petulant refusal to consider tradition at all and the self-mistrust that forbids the artist to look at his fellow's wares lest he be tempted overmuch to steal, result always in fumbling pretentiousness. For an artist to suppose that the discovery and practice of his forerunners can be neglected without disaster is to be duped, and to be tradition's dupe is no more admirable than to be its slave. Let us, before considering the real problem of the poet's proper relation to tradition and

[1] A paper read to the Royal Society of Literature.

the nourishment that he can draw from it, dismiss both slaves and dupes with a word or two. Of the slaves, indeed, hardly a word is necessary. The facile rhymesters who so copiously do ill what has already been done well are familiar to us all; their work is the token of half-witted appreciation of the work of others, and that is all there is to say. The dupes are not so easily measured. However far they may fall short of artistic salvation, they at least are not without artistic conscience. They do not understand; for they refuse the direction of an intelligence that is greater than theirs, the intelligence of generations, but their failure is one of undisciplined energy rather than of sloth. We are sometimes apt to be irritated by what seems to be the arrogance of these rather sorry tatterdemalions of art. Missing always the true significance of past achievement in their dread of its sorcery, they fall so often to abusing their fellows who, not fearing tradition, have mastered it. But it is, in truth, the abuse of unhappy minds, sick with half-realization of the health that they have missed. They remain inarticulate, and, unlike the slaves, not being withered in the roots, they know how desirable a thing articulation is. They are to be pitied, for there is no spiritual state so sorrowful as that of the man who, knowing, not as a delighted observer but with creative intensity, the beauty of expression, cannot achieve it. These men, scorning tradition, lose their birthright, and they know it; well may they watch with eager censoriousness for the lapses of those who have made the wiser choice. The nature of their loss we shall see in examining the true function of tradition in the poet's work.

We may consider the question in two phases — not, perhaps, philosophically separable, but conveniently assumed as such for our purpose; the poet's relation to tradition in manner on the one hand and in substance on the other. The latter is by far the subtler problem of the two, but commonly, when the subject is discussed, it is rather with reference to a poet's use or abuse of traditional verse forms or his revolt from them. Rebellion against metrical fitness has, I suppose, in every generation achieved as much notoriety as any other kind of lawlessness. We hear of it frequently enough to-day, and in the absence of any kindred manifestations commonly reported from the past, there are not wanting prophets who would persuade us that it is a new thing, a revolt long delayed but breaking at last against a manner that has already been too patiently tolerated and must now once and for all be discredited. The doctrine has a certain following, as every doctrine will always have that promises mastery without the pains of discipline. Destruction, it must be remembered, is a positive delight to many spirits to whom the joys of creation are sealed. Nothing is so comfortable to some minds as to contemplate the overthrow of beauty that jealously they do not understand, and to be assured that the measure is one of just reform, bringing an effete authority down from its pedestal, is to add a moral glow to an instinct immoral in essence. And so the gospel that the breaking of verse tradition is virtuous, and newly virtuous, is not altogether unprosperous. And yet we are sure that it has been advanced in every age with as much apparent credit, only its records have vanished as this later witness pathetically will vanish too. These arrogant but bewildered anarchs of earlier generations are nothing to-day but a stray note now and again in the second-hand-book catalogues, while the order against which they railed stands in proud achievement and in example that remains to-day a living influence upon all work that has in it promise of durability. For it is a very notable thing that every poet who has achieved unquestionable distinction has worked in forms that, even at the time of his writing, had a clearly recognizable parentage, while the rebels have achieved nothing. Whitman is the only possible exception, and his value is in spite of, and in no way because of, his manner. By rebels I mean the men who have, so to speak, been nonconformist to all the canons of poetic art that have been evolved, in England, through six centuries of practice, not the men who have explored and adapted those canons with every determination of creative energy; I mean the men who are radically insensible to the distinction between English prose and English verse. Rebellion in the finer sense of the word is as admirable in art as in any other form of activity, but in art, as in the State, there is a world of difference between the rebellion which is a protest against the abuse of government, a determination to restore government to decency and its right sphere of service, and anarchy, which is a protest against any government at all. It is true that every poet of distinction has refused to submit the subtleties of his own rhythmic sense to mere external rule, but it is equally and very splendidly true that every poet who has achieved mastery has found it not only possible but entirely satisfactory to himself to find infinite scope for the play of every rhythmic nicety to which his imagination moves within the confines of certain metrical structures that are the achievement of the cumulative poetic genius of his race. To take a simple and concrete example: it may be said that every poet, from Chaucer down to Rupert Brooke and his contemporaries, has done some of his best work in the five-foot iambic line that is the norm of English blank verse. A list of the poets of whom this is true would, I think, not exclude a single name of any importance. It is to be noted that the claim is not merely that every poet has used this form, but that every poet has achieved some of his best work in it. It is a simple fact which really disposes of the whole question of the fitness or otherwise of conformity to law in this matter. Here is a common verse unit which one poet after another for hundreds of years continues to find apt for his most personal and distinctive rhythmical needs. It would be absurd to suggest that his acceptance of it is mere laziness on his part; it can be due only to a profound and immutable rightness inherent in the form and approved with an ever-growing conviction by one generation of poets after another. And if the truth of this proposition be allowed, and I can see no escape from it, it is co-relatively true to say that the mood that acknowledges the fitness of a form that has, so to speak, universal authority, is not only a wholesome mood, but that it is the only wholesome mood, that it is an essential condition of full creative power, and that failure to realize this will inevitably result in an incurable formlessness which is the very antithesis of poetry, for poetry is, supremely, form.

We may, therefore, generalize in addition to our claim for the blank-verse line by saying that no truly memorable work can be achieved in a form that does not clearly bear the mark of its descent. And experience justifies the generalization in the most emphatic and unanswerable way. It is impossible to point to any notable English poem of which the metrical form is not demonstrably the offspring of a form already known. And to the possible objection that, while this has been so for five or six centuries, at length it is to-day no longer so, I can only answer that even to this immediate moment I find all the most interesting verse that is being written cast in established moulds. The newest poets represent a great variety of mood and poetic intention. But they are without exception agreed, in common with their fellows who already begin to belong not to the latest generation, in the use of metrical forms that frankly acknowledge their descent. No; the poet who thinks to prove his distinction by repudiating example instead of mastering it and using it with the freedom of mastery, proves nothing but his unfitness for the heritage, without which, in the light of strangely uniform experience, he cannot prosper. If a man cannot make, say, a five-foot iambic line his own, it means that he is not susceptible to the native properties of that line, and that means that he does not perceive a primary metrical characteristic of the language, and no amount of virtuosity in writing 'free verse' or 'prose poems' will redeem this cardinal defect in his equipment as a poet.

As a kind of intermediate step between metrical form and content matter we may consider diction. In the profounder sense diction is, perhaps, inseparable from content, since it is in the word that the intellectual perception is realized. But it is, I think, in this business of diction that the true poet is most likely to find himself in the toils with tradition. In his instinct about metrical form he may be relied on to keep, with but momentary lapses, a just balance between example and invention; he will find ample freedom in moving with his own modulations to measures which, in accepting them from the close deliberation of many ages, he truly discovers and recreates. Of his intellectual perceptions we may be equally assured, since the process of preparing these for poetic shape is so deliberate and intense that he cannot mistake what is stolen for his own without failing altogether to be a poet, and it is of the poet that we are speaking. But in his choice of diction he has not, in anything like the same degree, the guidance of a conditional instinct on the one hand, or of obvious obligation on the other, and it is here that he has to use his most unrelaxing wariness. The cumulative practice of poetry from one age to another creates a great volume of verbal expression that, having certain fundamental properties of fitness and passing into the common stock, makes the most seductive appeals to every new writer as he comes along. Upon the tact and wisdom with which he responds to these appeals, his success as a poet largely depends. To listen without discretion is quickly to become altogether insensible to the living qualities of language; to reject them out of hand is the same kind of error as his who thinks he can discard metrical tradition. This volume of expression may conveniently be divided into four groups, which may be called (*a*) description through salient qualities, (*b*) figures of speech, (*c*) images, (*d*) poetic conventions. As an example of description through salient quality let us take, very simply, 'the blue sky'; as an example of a figure of speech, 'he burns with rage'; of an image, 'the wings of time'; of a poetic convention, the use of 'thou' or 'thee' or 'thy' or 'thine' in any connection, or, more elaborately, such a phrase as 'methinks he hath a steed.' Of the first, second, and third of these exemplary phrases, it is immediately clear that they are in themselves notably appropriate and significant. Nothing is more profoundly and durably characteristic of the sky than its blueness; fire being the most fiercely consuming of the elements, what more natural when a man experiences so consuming an emotion as rage than to say that he burns with it? And since of all swift things nothing is so daily and beautifully present to our senses as the wings of a bird, and since of time we are conscious of nothing more urgently than its swift passing, to speak of the wings of time is to achieve finely imaginative truth at a word. Further, not only are these phrases appropriate and significant — they touch experience which everyone who considers the matter concerned with any intentness is very likely, if not certain, to realize for himself. A man can hardly think about the sky at all without thinking about its blueness; 'to burn with rage' is a figure that any poet might invent in the simplest process of his imagination, as he might associate the swift passing of time with flight and wings. Thus the poet, although he finds such phrases as these ready to his pen, may conceivably use them when his creative mood is active and not lethargic, and yet, unless he uses them with the greatest tact and economy, lethargy of the imagination will certainly be imputed to him, and it is a charge that carries conviction with it, against appeal. We find suggested here, indeed, a curiously subtle test of a poet's quality. It would be safe to say at a venture that every man who has written any considerable volume of verse has used, for example, the juxtaposition of 'blue' and 'sky,' and the decision as to whether we find in his use of the words personal vision or merely loose generalization, will be no negligible evidence as to the quality of his work as a whole. It is as fine a thing for the poet to call the sky blue because he is profoundly aware of its blueness, as it is weak of him to call it so because he has heard someone else doing so and he cannot think of anything else to say. And every reader of poetry knows how thrilling and newly charming such a phrase as 'the blue sky' may be in the hands of a

fine poet, how cloying when used by the lazy poet-
aster. Nevertheless, few, perhaps none, even of
the most vigilant poets are wholly blameless in this
matter; if any is, it is certain that here his vigilance
has been most closely exercised. Of the fourth
group, poetic conventions in diction, it need only
be observed that it is clearly ill-judged to perpetu-
ate in verse a manner of speech that once drew its
authority from the language of daily use but can
no longer do so. It was once in certain communities natural to say 'thou' and 'thee' instead of
'you,' but it is so no longer, just as it is mere at-
titudinizing to-day to say 'methinks he hath a
steed' instead of 'I think he has a horse,' while
once it was but to follow a common habit of
speech. It is an error to suppose that the language
of poetry should be the language of daily speech
and no more; it is the poet's business to create for
himself a speech that is a concentrated and quickened and enriched form of the speech that is habitual to the world in which he lives, but at the same
time it is essential, if his language is to have living
force, that it should not violate the idiom of common use by drifting into an outworn mode in the
delusion that to be detached and remote is to be
distinguished. To be detached in this kind is to
perish in an airless world. The word of poetry is
the fine flower of language, but the only soil from
which it can spring is the common speech of its

time. When a great poet like William Morris seems in his practice to deny this condition, it is but that he does in a particular and strangely impressive way actually live through his imagination in an age that is only not his own by an accident of time. And I do not think that his example can be matched.

The final aspect of my subject is, perhaps, the most important, since it concerns the origin of the poet's work — the content matter of his poetry. We touch at once a question upon which, I think, there is more misunderstanding in the approach to poetry than upon any other. In a world where the acquisition of knowledge is momently extolled as being commercially profitable, and where spiritual timidity is so prevalent that not one man in a hundred dare advance one step in his thought without a guide, poetry, like any other manifestation of individual life, is continually being tested by its power to tell us something that will help us towards solving the many riddles that perplex us as though we hoped that some day we might come upon a poet who should resolve the universe of our own spiritual experience into an exact and easy phrase. It is a test under which poetry inexorably refuses to reveal its secret. And yet this content matter, this opinion, far from being of little moment to the poet himself, must absorb and compel his whole being, or his poetry can come to nothing.

It is a strangely impressive operation of the nature of poetry (of all art, it might be said), that what the poet says is the source and condition of every virtue that his work may have, and is yet, if we are truly prepared for the high grace that poetry can bestow upon us, a thing in itself of no concern for us. For the value of the poet's work to us lies not in the nature of the thing that he sees, but in the intensity of his vision. Nearly all the nonsense that is talked about art springs from the preposterous and idle claim that the artist should confirm our own impressions or elucidate our difficulties. We have not begun to perceive the virtue of art until we know that the artist's sole duty towards us is so to quicken our own faculties by contact with his that they shall move with new power and assurance to the shaping of our own vision, to the ease of our own speculation. This being so, it follows that to demand of the poet that his meditation should chiefly touch the questions that are peculiarly of his own time, is to ask him to do work for us that we ought to do for ourselves, and to pay no respect to the nature of his art. When we say that a poet ought to be concerned with contemporary life, we have no right to mean more than that he should so keep his faculties in touch with the men and women and phenomena of his daily experience as to bring the warm glow of reality into his work by the contact. We should mean, for example, that

if he is singing to-day the beauty of Helen of Troy
he should have thrilled to the beauty of some Helen
of Liverpool or the Old Kent Road, or that if he
recalls the coming of Persephone he should have
gone delightedly himself through spring meadows.
It may, indeed, be dangerous for him to use the
machinery of an age not his own, since it is easier
then for him to lapse from direct realization of his
subject into the easy acceptance of another man's
presentment. But his choice in this is his own affair,
to justify or not as he can, and in experience we
find the poets in all ages freely using not only the
habit and event of an earlier day as the body that
is to be informed with their own meditation upon
life, but we frequently find them using this habit
and event not merely as they stand in the un-
shaped condition of barely recorded facts, but as
they have already been projected through another
artist's mind. That they often improve upon their
sources is but a happy accident of genius. Shakespeare borrowing extant plays and romances and
chronicles and working to their pattern often with
the most literal fidelity, Keats brooding over
'Paradise Lost' in preparation for 'Hyperion,'
Morris retelling the Northern sagas and the stories
of the classic and romantic worlds, Mr. Yeats re-
creating the legends of heroic Ireland, Mr. Hardy
using the text-books of Napoleonic history for his
great epic-drama as strictly as though he were

about to take his final schools, Burns making songs out of songs already made, Mr. Lascelles Abercrombie finding his new world in the Bible, and all of them achieving masterpieces stamped with their own personality in the process — these are instances, to which any number could be added, of the unquestioning readiness of the poet to use a traditional world as the agent or fable of his subject-matter. And it must be remembered that when his information about this traditional world comes not from another poet, but from the relatively unimpassioned records of history, nevertheless it is still touched with something of the recorder's personality, differentiating it by so much from the actual life that is under his own direct observation and between which and his own vision no other mind intervenes. The reason why the traditional world may, in spite of this, remain as fruitful for his purpose as the world of daily affairs in which he moves is that, before he can succeed as a poet, he has to re-create his material in the light of his own vision as much in one case as the other, and the whole value of his work lies in this act of re-creation. It is really not in the smallest degree easier for a man to-day to see a motor-bus in Oxford Street with any personal and vivid realization than it is for him so to see a chariot in the streets of imperial Rome. The point is that if he has been able to see the bus with any sharpness of impression, the ex-

perience will enable him to see the chariot in the
same way, while if the bus has gone by and he has
had no such experience, then he can know nothing
more of the chariot than he may learn with the
mind of the duller antiquarian. If, possessed of the
faculty of seeing, he chooses to write about the bus,
it is clearly the very inanity of criticism that com-
plains that a bus is not a poetical subject; but if,
with his faculty alert from immediate experience,
he realizes the chariot and chooses to write about
that, it is equally inane to say that this is not a
subject of contemporary interest. When the poet
has proved his power of personal realization, we
have no right to make further conditions, for he
can prove this only by bringing to the shaping of
his subject, whatever it may be, the intensity born
of his own contact with reality. Nor should it be
forgotten that any man's direct experience of actual
event is extremely limited, and to suggest that the
artist should confine himself to such experience is
to suggest that his art should be cut off from what
is often the greater part of the most fertile material
upon which his mind can work. What we know of
event by report is at least as important in itself
as what we know by observation. It is, indeed,
through observed event that our perceptive faculties are trained, and it is a mistake to say that a
poet is of limited power because, as sometimes
happens (Mr. W. H. Davies is a notable instance in

our own day), he rarely goes beyond the very limited range of observed event for his material, being at the same time justly content to make no effort to extend that range. He may in such a case sound as clear and deep and true a note as another poet who explores every possible variety of event, and just as it is a fallacy to suppose that you can learn more of human nature by travelling the world than you can in your own street, so it is a fallacy to suppose that Byron magnificently sweeping the landscape of Europe into his verses is nearer to the heart of nature, and speaking with profounder knowledge, than John Clare when he sings, season by season, half a dozen Northamptonshire fields. But most temperaments, having developed the perceptive faculty by exercising it upon event arising in their own direct experience, are eager to apply it to a wider range of event. The difference between the two kinds of temperament is, perhaps, a psychological obscurity into which nothing would be gained by inquiring; in any case, the fact that it exists is all that is to the present purpose. And in absorbing this event that comes to it by report, the perceptive faculty may work as significantly as in its realization of the event in its own direct experience. The poet, his mind alert, may be as truly moved by a friend's recital of experience as by any adventure of his own. And if the poet may thus respond to contemporary report which, however crude it is, must nevertheless have moved some degree along the process of shaping the raw material of experience, with what reason can we ask him to be deaf to that other and greater world of report which is history and legend or these things transmuted by poets who have gone before him? If he cannot distinguish between using this recorded experience as material for his own art and the clumsy pretence that the art by which that experience has been recorded is his own, he is fatally defective as a poet, but it is absurd to make the danger of such failure a pretext for forbidding to the poet what amounts to far the greater part of all accessible experience. All we have to do is to be sure that the faculty of experiencing is his own; for the rest, he must be free to range where he will in its exercise.

We have considered the metrical form, the diction, and the subject-matter of poetry in their relation to tradition. There remains one more question, or, perhaps, it is rather another aspect of the last of these three considerations, namely, whether poetry is in danger of falling into a dully conventional manner of approach to its subject-matter. Take, for example, that perennial source of poetry, the Spring. If we allow that the poet may select the flowers and buds and bird-song of April as a fitting subject for his poetry, that he may celebrate them in a metrical form that, being traditional, is yet alive with his individual rhythmic sense, and that while he is inventing a diction of his own, a distribution of words that is witness to his own subtle perception of the life that is in them, he may still call the fields green or the sky blue or the birds happy without wholly forfeiting his claim to distinction, is there not yet something false in the reiteration with which one poet after another tells us that his mood in perceiving this phenomenon of Spring is one of mysterious excitement and elation? Is not this as much a conceit of the mind as, say, the conventional daily pretence that we are anxious about the health of acquaintances in whom we have not the smallest personal interest? Does not the poet, in fact, profess this mood of elation because it is the traditional habit of poets to do so? I have chosen a very simple example, which may be said to answer itself, and yet in its character it touches an important and much misunderstood poetic principle. The poet is often subjected to angry criticism because the mood in which he considers his subject-matter is one already commonly used on like occasion. The answer to the charge is that a mood is no more the peculiar province of an individual poet than the common metrical resources and the words of his language or the general stock of human experience can be, and that, like these, his mood, whatever its colour may be, becomes interesting for us if in his expression of it he convinces us not that it is a new mood, but that he has truly informed it with his own consciousness. It is conceivable that a man should be dejected by the coming of Spring, but it is undoubted that nearly all men are in fact elated. And it is idle to ask that the poet should prove his distinction by finding some new mood in which to contemplate the Spring. What we want him to do is to convince us of the elation that he feels, no matter though a thousand poets have felt elation at the same experience before. As I say, in so simple an example the truth of the conclusion is self-evident; yet the poet is in effect too often scolded for not being moved at the approach of Spring by anger, or fear, or indignation, or some other such original and inappropriate emotion.

It may be interesting, before leaving the subject, to examine a single short passage in the light of the views advanced. A dozen lines from a poem of Marvell, the most famous lines of an acknowledged masterpiece, will, I think, illustrate every condition of my argument:

> 'But at my back I always hear
> Time's winged chariot hurrying near,
> And yonder all before us lie
> Deserts of vast eternity.
> Thy beauty shall no more be found,
> Nor, in thy marble vault, shall sound
> My echoing song; then worms shall try
> That long-preserved virginity,

> And your quaint honour turn to dust,
> And into ashes all my lust.
> The grave's a fine and private place,
> But none, I think, do there embrace.'

Here, in the first place, is a verse-measure that had already in Marvell's time long been established in English poetry, and yet how subtly in every phrase does it respond to a new imagination working at high creative pressure.

> 'But at my back I always hear
> Time's winged chariot hurrying near,
> And yonder all before us lie
> Deserts of vast eternity.'

Every beat of it is nervous with Marvell's own rhythmic sense. We observe, too, that there is no anxiety to avoid the traditional devices in diction of which we have spoken. We find almost the very phrases that have been mentioned. Not the 'blue sky,' but 'vast eternity' serves as well, and then we have 'Time's winged chariot,' and lust turning to ashes, which means that the lover 'burns with love' only instead of the 'burns with rage' of our instance. 'Thou' was more fitly used three hundred years ago than it is now, but even Marvell is hesitant about it, since he uses both 'thy' and 'your' in the same passage. And yet, notwithstanding all this simple readiness to accept tradition, with what superb mastery does the whole diction become the poet's own creation:

>   ... then worms shall try
> That long-preserved virginity,
> And your quaint honour turn to dust,
> And into ashes all my lust. ·
> The grave's a fine and private place,
> But none, I think, do there embrace.

This is truly lordship of the word. Finally, there is the subject-matter; the lover's exhortation to his mistress merely not to let youth go by unfulfilled. The lover's mind since lost antiquity had so been preoccupied before Marvell, and yet, again, how brightly the experience flows anew under this vivid faculty of experiencing; and the mood in which the experience is approached is that one of gallant and passionate intensity of persuasion that is almost universally common to the occasion, but it is that mood made this poet's own with immortal distinction. They are not careful overmuch, these poets, of the dangers of tradition; they can dare to profit by its service, for they are armed by their own vitality against its domination.

'SIMPLE, SENSUOUS, AND PASSIONATE'

I wandered lonely as a cloud
    That floats on high o'er vales and hills,
When all at once I saw a crowd,
    A host of golden daffodils;
Beside the lake, beneath the trees,
Fluttering and dancing in the breeze.

Continuous as the stars that shine
    And twinkle on the milky way,
They stretched in never-ending line
    Along the margin of a bay;
Ten thousand saw I at a glance,
Tossing their heads in sprightly dance.

The waves beside them danced; but they
    Outdid the sparkling waves in glee;
A poet could not but be gay
    In such a jocund company;
I gazed — and gazed — but little thought
What wealth the show to me had brought:

For oft, when on my couch I lie
    In vacant or in pensive mood,
They flash upon that inward eye
    Which is the bliss of solitude;
And then my heart with pleasure fills,
And dances with the daffodils.

WORDSWORTH, *The Daffodils*

THE more we consider the nature of poetry, the
more adequate and precise does Milton's stipula-
tion appear. It must, we remember, be simple, sensuous, and passionate, conditions which Coleridge
elaborates, not unhelpfully, thus — single in con-

ception, abounding in sensible images, and informing them all with the spirit of the mind. To take
these essential qualities and refer them to the poem
that we are considering: 'simple,' it seems to me,
implies not only singleness of conception, but also
a corresponding singleness of expression; it denotes,
in fact, the achievement of the artistic form that
conveys complete perception from one mind to
another, and, as it is a condition that relates to the
finished poem with all its contributory parts, it may
best, I think, be considered last instead of first, as
Milton puts it. First, then, we are told that it
must be sensuous, or abounding in sensible images.
The virtue of an image to the poet's reader is that
it forces his mind in the most direct manner to an
unembarrassed act of creation, to a motion having
something of the lucid vitality that is the poet's
own. It is always possible for us to see a thing with
the physical eye dully, without any consequent act
of sharp mental realization. But when a poet sees a
thing with sufficient intensity to translate it from
its own natural expression to a mental image recorded in words, he not only proves his own realization of the object, but makes it imperative that
we, in reading his words, shall perform an act of
realization ourselves or get from him nothing but
empty sound. So communicative of life is the poet's
created image of a natural object, that many
minds, while they are still relatively insensitive to

the natural object in itself, respond to the poet's realization of it with a realization of their own. This mental state of realization, it must be noted in passing, is altogether more vivid than that of mere appreciation. Few people would be likely to see a blowing bed of daffodils at a lakeside without some heightening of emotion; but even fewer, perhaps, would see it with that quickening of formal vision which it is the highest of our hopes to foster, since it is the condition of understanding, of justice. When, however, we see nothing with the physical eye, but read of

> 'A host of golden daffodils;
> Beside the lake, beneath the trees,
> Fluttering and dancing in the breeze,

we either perform a complete act of mental realization or we experience nothing at all. The image that is before us cannot be perceived with the blurred appreciation through which we may so easily see the natural object; if it exists for us at all it exists lucidly, completely. Although the philosophers may tell us that the natural object cannot exist apart from the beholding mind, it is clear that it may be beholden by a succession of minds without inducing any vivid realizing movement in one of them; but those lines of the poet cannot operate in this way, since either they convey nothing, or the mind in perceiving the image that is created in them is really perceiving an image that it has itself created. There is another example of this direct imaging in Wordsworth's poem:

> 'Ten thousand saw I at a glance,
> Tossing their heads in sprightly dance.'

But the image in poetry sometimes fulfils a more complex function than this. The stimulus of mind such as is received from the creation of a simple image, as those just mentioned, becomes yet greater and subtler when the process is the dual one of perceiving the image of one natural object through the creation of that of another. When the mind performs this act of co-relating the unrelated [1] it is being educated for its most fruitful activity, and it is the poet who most habitually helps us towards this liberation. The poet presents to us two separate simple images, 'I wandered lonely,' and 'a cloud that floats on high o'er vales and hills.' Each has an independent being, and before we can proceed to understanding of his thought, we have to re-create each of them separately in our own mind. But his concern at the moment is with the fact of his loneliness; and to express this with the greatest possible force, he states it first in one simple image, then creates another and wholly unrelated image, carries over our attention from the governing idea of

[1] I owe this admirable phrase to my friend, Mr. H. P. Morrison. Whether he invented it or discovered it in the depths of his French learning, I do not know, but it is too good not to steal as readily as if it were the commonplace of criticism that it deserves to be.

loneliness in the first image to this particular characteristic of the second, and applies it back again to the original conception upon which it operates with enormously increased intensity. Thus, again, in

> 'The waves beside them danced; but they
> Outdid the sparkling waves in glee . . .'

and, very splendidly, in —

> 'Continuous as the stars that shine
> And twinkle on the milky way,
> They stretched in never-ending line
> Along the margin of a bay. . . .'

This, then, is what we mean when we say that a poem should be sensuous or abounding with sensible images, and we see the value that this quality has in bracing our minds. We may now examine what is meant by the claim that a poem should, further, be passionate, or, as Coleridge says, informed throughout with the spirit of the mind.[1]

By passionate, it must be remembered, we mean something more than emotional intensity. Coleridge reminds us that the word, as Milton uses it, implies an intellectual quality, a power, beyond the translation of the vivid perception into an image, of giving a whole poetic conception intel-

---

[1] I do not think that it necessarily follows that because these demands that Milton makes must be met before a poem can be acclaimed as satisfying us in all respects, a poem that disregards one or another of them must be wholly a failure.

lectual stability, of informing it, as it were, not only with sensitiveness but also with the proportions of lucid thought. It is a common error to think of the intellect as being cold and dry, an energy with which poetry should have as little to do as possible. The fact is, however, that while poetry may achieve durable charm without this quality, which is in effect what Rossetti called fundamental brain-work, no poetry of the highest order does exist without it.

It often happens that a young poet, in the first flush of his poetic sensibility, enchants us by the very rapture of imaginative experience through which he is passing, but it is not until he has been working for some years that we are able to tell whether he has the profounder gift of transforming intellectual power into passion. If he does not develop this faculty the result is inevitably a barren maturity following upon a rapidly exhausted flight of early song. Wagner spoke wisely when he said that before he could tell whether a man was truly a poet he must know whether he could sing when he was forty. We have known instances in our time of poets who have thus disappointed enthusiastic and reasonable hope. The reaction that has followed upon the excited applause that greeted the work of such a poet as Stephen Phillips has been bitter in proportion to the exaggeration of the welcome. But the one is unjustified and cruel as the other was unjustified and hysterical. Phillips's early work had, and will always retain, an undeniable charm. That it clearly echoed the work of other poets is no condemnation, since as much may be said of the early work of any of the masters. Here was a poetic sensitiveness, ardent, sufficiently personal to make its own ventures, provoking in the poet an acute sense of a certain stiff verbal beauty, and communicating delight to any ungrudging reader. But there was behind its sensitiveness no intellectual staying power, and, once the charming energy of youth had spent itself, there was no more durable faculty waiting to exercise the poet's gift.

Perhaps the most notable instance in our own time of a poet who has, on the other hand, shown this development from the poetry of enchanting sensibility to that of intellectual passion is to be found in Mr. W. B. Yeats. It is instructive, as showing the relative inability of readers who respond readily enough to the slighter graces of poetry to appreciate the profounder beauty of this passion, to hear it said, as it often is, that this poet's later work lacks the enchantment of his earlier. To a right understanding, Mr. Yeats's work has grown steadily in significance from the first, and this because of its surely maturing brain work. In Wordsworth's poem, simple in occasion as it is, we have this quality working with steady incandescence. Down to the second line of the third stanza we have a perfectly shaped statement and elaboration of the image, growing in intensity to the marvellous figure of the flowers outdoing the sparkling waves in glee. So far we have, created by a consummate master, that essential part of poetry which is so championed by certain writers in these later days who, while they do well enough to remind us of an eternal necessity, seem, by their assumption of the title *imagiste*, to forget that their aim has been part of the aim of every poet of consequence since the beginning. But it is at this point that Wordsworth shows us that the poet's business does not end with the creation of an image, but that he must go beyond this to the application of his image to requirements of profound and governing thought. It is here that perhaps the poet's greatest danger lies, and his greatest glories for the winning. Merely to make his creation the occasion for some trite moral reflection is to debase his art and waste our time. What he has to do is so to focus his intellect upon the image that he has created as to be able not only to make us realize the image itself, but also to perceive with passionate understanding the significance of that image in the whole texture of our lives. We may observe then with what exquisite precision Wordsworth achieves this end. First he tells us that he could not but be gay in such a jocund company, then that he was receiving some virtue without knowing what it was:

'I gazed — and gazed — but little thought
What wealth the show to me had brought.'

Then, in the last stanza, with that lucidity to
which the whole difficult world of the brain is
touched in rare moments at the great artist's bidding, we have the philosophical application of the
poetic conception made, and made, in Milton's
full use of the word, passionately:

'For oft, when on my couch I lie
    In vacant or in pensive mood,
They flash upon that inward eye
    Which is the bliss of solitude;
And then my heart with pleasure fills,
And dances with the daffodils.'

This is a perfect example of Coleridge's 'informing all with the spirit of the mind.' Its value to us
as readers cannot be set too highly. Poetry which
freely complies with this demand rescues the
artist's office finely from the last possible designs
of the dilettante mind which, at the risk of falling
away altogether from life, supposes that the creation of an image is a sufficient end in itself. To be
dilettante in the arts is, indeed, more admirable
than to be pedestrian, but the artist who has any
understanding of his responsibility refuses one
course no less than the other.

We have finally to consider the quality of simplicity which Milton places first among his conditions of poetry. The fundamental obligation of the

poet to translate the formlessness of life into intelligible form for our understanding must not be confused, as it often is, with the banal statement in lifeless terms of generalizations with which we are already familiar. For example, we all know as a matter of workaday experience that a charge to goodness, at the expense if need be of cleverness, is sound enough in itself. But when Kingsley [1] says,

'Be good, sweet maid, and let who will be clever,'

he is not being simple in any real poetic sense, but merely playing up to the platitude that is already established in our minds, and relying upon that for his effect and not upon any creative perception of his own.

He is, profoundly, not being simple at all in the way that Milton means. He is, rather, setting down an obvious and widely current conclusion of an extremely complex and difficult psychological question, the obscure nature of which he leaves untouched. The simplicity by which the poet gains distinction is that which seizes some illusive operation of the mind upon natural objects and so expresses it that what was incomprehensible to us before becomes suddenly defined. In other words, the poet must make a simple statement, but it must be a statement of something that without his vision

---

[1] My use of Kingsley as an example in this connection does not lessen my admiration for the poet of *The Sands of Dee*.

must have remained dark and formless. Nothing could be more superbly simple, for example, than

> 'Nothing extenuate
> Nor set down aught in malice; then must you speak
> Of one that loved not wisely but too well.'

But in two lines here is recorded a whole voyage of psychological insight. It may be added that since no experience is ever final, an endless succession of poets may bring simplicity to the same preoccupation, and each give us delight and satisfaction in turn. Even the same poet may do this himself on many occasions:

> 'This life is but a shadow, a poor player
> That struts and frets his hour upon the stage
> And then is heard no more.'

And again:

> 'We are such stuff
> As dreams are made of and our little life
> Is rounded with a sleep.'

And again:

> 'Golden lads and girls all must
> As chimney sweepers come to dust.'

And yet again:

> 'Since brass, nor stone, nor earth, nor boundless sea
> But sad mortality o'ersways their power.'

And lastly, to give but one more of the numerous examples which Shakespeare alone might supply:

'Of all the wonders that I have yet heard,
It seems to me most strange that men should fear;
Seeing that death, a necessary end,
Will come when it will come.'

In Wordsworth's 'Daffodils' we have a remarkable instance of this first necessity in poetry.
The poem in its meaning is clear for any reader.
We leave it with a perfectly formed realization,
reached through a sharply defined and particular
instance, of the pleasure that may come to us from
remembered moments of ecstatic experience. But
we are made free of this simplicity of perception
only through this subtle psychological analysis on
the part of the poet. The phrase,

'They flash upon that inward eye
Which is the bliss of solitude,'

is magnificent in its simplicity, because the phenomenon which is here reduced to plain terms is not
one of simple appearance in itself, but so intricate
that for all the tens of millions of people who had
experienced it not one before Wordsworth had been
able to arrest it with the perfect touch of definition.
Of the value for us which this quality gives to
poetry it need only be said that without it we can
understand nothing, or at most something which
is not worth our understanding; with it every true
poem is treasure trove for us, giving us that rarest
spiritual satisfaction which we experience when
we can suddenly resolve obscurity, and know our

minds liberated from confusion. We may now summarize the impression that Wordsworth's poem yields to alert reading, thus: our perceptions are quickened by having to create images to correspond to those created by the poet. These quickened senses are then directed by the poet's intellectual passion to a relation of these particular images to a presiding vision of life and experience. Then, by the primary creative act of the poet, the bringing of material into shape, these processes of our mind become definable in our own consciousness: are complete.

POETRY AND CONDUCT

WHEN every philosophy has been tested, when all policies have been heard and all speculations as to the destiny of man weighed one against another, it is bigotry alone that will assert that it has the last word in any argument. No social faith is ever wholly proved, there is no god but will sooner or later be dethroned, no chart of life that we can know with certainty is truly drawn. This is not unhappily so. The imagination of man is so vast an instrument, and the world of experience upon which it may work so varied and so exhilarating, that a lifetime of untiring activity will enable us at best to realize but an odd stray here and there from the thronging life that is daily waiting to be shaped to our delight. The man who is continually refusing the witness of his own imagination and is crying for the assurance of authorities other than his own alert spirit is withered in the centre, he is spiritually dead. You may be sorry for him; his misfortune may be explained. Life may have dealt so hardly with him, his nature may be so little robust or may have been so ill-tended, that he cannot oppose calamity with the resources of his own resilient character and imagination. But compassion and a recognition of causes do not alter the fact that here is spiritual death — the most lamentable, as it is, perhaps, the commonest of all tragedies. It is a tragedy that permeates society, thriving even when there is no bitter burden of cruel experience to excuse or at least to explain it. Flourishing trades are built upon it. We all know the unfortunate people whose spiritual lethargy is so profound, who are so insensible to the calls of the innumerable adventures that are in every wind and bough and footstep, that they will pay sly palmists to tell them of a to-morrow that they may be sure will be duller than to-day. It is a tragedy that our newspapers exploit with a certain knowledge of profit. So general is the apathy in which we move that a placard promising us a sensation — it is the very word of common use — will sell a paper to three men out of four as they pass.

This pervading dulness of spirit is the gravest penalty that we pay for an over-specialized civilization. There are so many things that, in the state which we have blindly chosen, have to be done by routine and example, that routine and example have become habits with us, creeping from what should be their lowly station of servility and warping the free functions of our imagination. That this should be so is tragic chiefly because it is a denial of our proudest right. If absolute knowledge is beyond our attainment, as it is, a continuity of vivid experience is not beyond our attainment, and such activity of experience is the fulfilment of the highest function of which man is capable. It is health; it is peace — the peace that passeth all understanding, that is, the peace that is greater than all understanding. Its full and perfect realization is, perhaps, impossible, but that it can be realized in some measure is the hope, indeed the certainty, that makes this perplexing and capricious life so greatly worth living. That this experience includes sorrow does not affect the question. It is the act of experiencing that matters, that exercises our nature in the only full and significant way. And out of this exercise, this alertness of our nature, which is in and for itself of supreme importance to us as individuals, comes a sure and single sense of justice, which is of equal importance to us as members of society. For all injustice, and injustice is the only social evil, or we may say that it covers all social evils, is born of spiritual lethargy. When a man's thought is alert, when his spirit is responsive to the beauty and awe of the world, he does not put his hand to the terrible evil of injustice.

For its direct value to us, then, as individuals, liberating as it does the highest force that is in us, and for its indirect influence upon our social integrity, this wealth of passionate experience is the thing that we must most desire. To destroy lethargy of spirit, to shape all our daily meditation and intercourse and the fertile activity of the natural world into sharp and intimately realized forms in our own imagination, is the aim of every rightly disciplined mind. And in the accomplishment of this aim the poet is he who of all men can give us the surest help. Without inquiring too curiously whether the desire for this intensity of experience can in the beginning come from any external impulse, whether it must not at first make some unaided gesture, it is not questionable that once it has moved, however shyly, contact with fine poetry will of all things foster it into vigorous certainty and growth. For contact with fine poetry is precisely contact with most vital and personal experience conveyed to us in the most persuasive medium invented by man for habitual intercourse — pregnant and living words. Pregnant and living: for here is the secret of poetry. The use of words, in the common run of daily affairs, has become so much a matter of habit, so dependent upon the thousand small conventions by which we conduct the necessary or chosen routine of our lives, that it is devoid of any real significance. The common use of words is to convey from one man to another information, which is a thing quite distinct from experience, since we have trained ourselves to receive and impart a great deal of information daily out of mere custom and for the purpose of keeping pace with the exacting and often monstrous machinery that governs our society. If we could number the words passing to and from us in the course of a week that were really born of significant and urgent experience, we should have but a very small reckoning. And, not being born of this quick experience seeking to announce itself, the words are not pregnant and living, but dead. Most of the multitudes of words that are current among us have no true significance at all. I do not say that they are not necessary, or that it would be possible for men to bear the pressure of constant interchange of words that had real significance, but the fact is, none the less, that words as we continually use them for the common purposes of daily traffic mean, in the more exacting sense, nothing. It is only when they are used to convey experience that they become quick and stir in us not a mere acceptance that is barely a mental action at all, but an energy of experience that corresponds to the energy that is their source. And it is of the necessity that such experience finds, when it is most profound, to state itself in perfectly selected and ordered words, that poetry comes into being. The precision and light that are the characteristics of fine poetry can be achieved by intense and individual experience and from no other source whatever. This is not to say that intensity and individuality of experience are in themselves enough to create poetry; the poet alone knows the diligence with which he must discipline his craftsmanship before he can serve his art worthily. But they are none the less the only sources of the material upon which he can hopefully direct his craftsmanship; it is from them alone that his words win their significance, and it is of them that his words speak to us, compelling in us an ecstasy which is exactly a response to that ecstasy of his own. And so it is that he, of all external influences, is the most potent in directing us to the realization of what should be our deepest desire, spiritual activity.

So do we trace the association, profound and of far greater importance than is ever realized in the government of the world, between poetry and conduct. The old question as to whether poetry — or any art — should proclaim a moral can occupy none but dull and unimaginative minds. Poetry proclaims life; that is all and it is everything. Didactic poetry does not necessarily fail. It generally does so, and because it generally comes not of conviction, not of that urgent experience, but of the lethargic acceptance of this or that doctrine or moral attitude that is not the poet's own delighted discovery, and so we respond to it with no more than lethargic acceptance on our side. It is always a question of the poet's sincerity and conviction. Our experience in receiving his poetry must correspond to his experience in creating it, and it is experience alone that we demand of it. What the nature of the experience is does not matter, but the experience itself must be thrilling with life. This question was raised aptly enough at a debate recently in one of our universities, when a motion was put that 'the trend of modern drama is and should be sociological and not poetic.' That is to say, what is poetical is not sociological. I can only see one possible way of reasoning whereby so queer a conclusion can have been reached. Sociology, it must have been argued, is a practical science, concerned directly with the practical conditions of our daily lives. And then, it must have been said, poetry is something which is not so concerned. And a convenient popular fallacy was ready to hand in support of the notion. For is not the poet a vague and ambitious visionary, creating in his fancy a pleasant world of retreat from the unfortunate difficulties of actual life? Does not poetry, therefore, bear the mark of its makers, being the fit concern only of people who are prepared to shut their eyes to the distressing phenomena which vex the routine of our busy days? Yes, yes — it is consoling enough at stray moments when the armour is off to indulge in this pleasant pilgrimage to Lotus-Land, leaving the fret and burden of affairs, of the great problems of evolution, behind us. They are good fellows, these poets, in their way, giving us enchanting interludes of make-believe against the sterner business of life. But, remember, we are serious men and women in our normal hours, facing this great seething perplexity with stubborn wills to master it if we can, and we want our drama to be serious in its aim too, to become the powerful pulpit that it may be, pointing us shortly to answering these many questions that beset us, or, better still, answering them for us outright. The poets — yes, on dreamy afternoons when, tired and dusty from the momentous struggles that are our daily use, we snatch an hour's well-earned idleness; even, in strictly governed measure, and if it be not too difficult, as a diversion from the more important matter of our morning papers. But in the theatre? No, not for two hours and a half when we would settle our minds to grave and more responsible things.

This is, unhappily, no fantastic manipulating of a case. This fundamental misunderstanding of the nature of poetry is common enough in the world, as, if it would but see it, Europe to-day should realize. Our governors have not taken art, which is spiritual activity with its consequent clear-sighted moral judgment, seriously, and we and our governors are paying the sorry penalty. But let us think a little more of that curious proposition. What is the purpose of sociology? Is it anything more or less than the better regulation of society, which is the relationship of man to his fellows? That is what all your sociologists are striving for, unless they are lost in a mere maze of

theories. We are gregarious cattle, and we do not
very well know how to behave to each other at all
times. Quite simply, as I have already said, we are
unjust to one another. The sociologist examines
the phenomena of this injustice in the abstract,
tabulates the results, underlines as far as may be
the points at which reform may most hopefully
make its attacks, and suggests the methods by
which such reforms should work. Admirable: full
of fine zeal, often even of heroism. And your sociological dramatist, yet more sensitive to the grievous
manifestations of this injustice, defines them yet
more clearly through the agency of imagined men
and women. Yet more admirable, striking as it does
more directly at the heart. But, when all is said, all
these people — the people among whom sociological
inquiry and enthusiasm take the form of a definite
exposure of particular social injustice — are but
telling us what we know. And here is the centre of
the matter. I do not say that it is not a good thing
to tell us what we know. I do not say that if you
tell us often and eloquently enough you will not
sometimes shame us into sudden resolutions that
may bear fruit in some actual reparation, but I do
say that to tell us what we know is not at all the
same or so big a thing as to make us order that
knowledge in our minds with a clear moral judgment. If, for example, you take your industrial
sweater, and ask him over his lunch whether he

thinks it good to steal another man's labour and food and life itself, he will tell you — no. He knows it is evil, but he does not mind evil. And you may demonstrate as clearly and as persuasively as you will to him in propaganda or on the stage or from the pulpit that this sweating is evil, and you will only have told him what he knew, and still he will not mind evil. You have done nothing to rouse him from the lethargy of spirit which is the cause of his insensibility to the ugliness of the evil that he does.

This lethargy comes of too close a preoccupation with facts. To be a man of affairs — and we are all in some measure men of affairs — generally means a too constant absorption in facts for any concern with what is really important, the significance of facts. Again, the newspapers, those great criterions of popular temper, flatter, sagely enough, a characteristic which is so general. They will tell us that a wretched clerk has defrauded his employers of five pounds, and that he has been sent to prison for two years, knowing that the public is greedy for facts. But what are we told of the significance of these facts, of the surrounding circumstances, of the conflict of mind and the failure of character, of the hearts that must bear the punishment without having offended, of the wreckage of love, of the petty and odious tyrannies that have made trouble yet more difficult? Nothing; for we have no taste for these things, our spirits being inactive, not

eager for experience. And our industrial sweater —
a single practitioner in the evil of injustice of which
we are none of us blameless, none of us being always and wholly free of this lethargy — living dully
under this deadening pressure of facts, has not the
spiritual wit to realize that the evil which he does
is a terrible thing. He knows that it is evil, but he
does not feel its terror. If, as I have said, you show
him its terror very vividly and directly in your
drama or otherwise, you may occasionally shock
him into perception, but in nearly every case the
shock will be merely temporary and effect no
radical quickening of the spirit. And it is just such
radical quickening of the spirit which is the only
effective cure for injustice of all kinds, and, as we
have seen, it is just this radical quickening of
the spirit which is the highest function of poetry.
The poet will commonly, in the intensity of his
vision, see beyond the facts of our immediate concern as sociologists into the great eternal assertion
of which these are but local and ever mutable nega-
tions. He will — not necessarily, but commonly —
sing humanity with all its natural sorrows and exultations, without emphasizing this or that particular folly which is only of particular application.
And in doing this (let me here say that nothing is
easier than for a man to deceive himself that he is
doing this when he is doing no more than to repeat
a bundle of hearsay generalities about which he has

no real conviction whatever, and so to become that most troublesome and useless of all things — a pseudo-poet) the poet, whether we agree with what he has to say or not, quickens our imaginative perception. That is to say, he makes us alive. And, quite definitely, to be alive is to be moral. Injustice is the result of mental inertia; that is to say that unjust people, in so far as they are unjust, are spiritually dead people.

Remembering always that the chief distinction of poetry is that it enables men who are habitually responsive to its appeal to exult in the beauty and the heroic conflict of life, and that this other virtue, this conditioning of men's minds so that injustice becomes abhorrent, is but its secondary glory, this is the case for poetry as a sociological weapon and as the most wholesome of all influences upon conduct; being the expression of the most intense spiritual activity to which man can attain, it, more than any other use of the common means of communication, words, begets spiritual activity in its hearers. And to combat the supreme evil of society, injustice, we need not be told that it is evil, which we know and yet persist in its practice, but to have our spiritual activity quickened, when we shall know that it is loathsome, and crush it.

Of the three principal elements of poetry as it leaves the poet a finished art, rhythm, diction, and the image, the one having the most immediate and widest appeal is rhythm with its emphasis, rhyme. Consequently, since the capacity for rhyme and simple rhythm is common, these are the qualities which are most frequently abused and in themselves mistaken for poetry when the finer spirit of poetry has left them untouched. Simple rhythms have been and are continually used by poets to contain the rarest poetic imagination, but in themselves they may be ordered by the most unpoetic minds to no better purpose than pointing reflections that have neither savour nor persuasion, and minds equally barren of imaginative fervour will give these jingles glad acceptance as shaping, a little more clearly than they have done for themselves, their own jaded moralities. And so it is that what passes for poetry is widely extolled as the most efficient of all guides to conduct by people who have in their hearts no tidings whatever of poetry and its functions. I have a little book which, although it belongs to an earlier generation, would, I am sure, find a large public to-day if its Victorian dress were remodelled to our later modes. It is called 'Learning to Converse,' and it has two splendidly instructive chapters on poetry. An impeccable uncle is teaching his nephew, Edmund, the art of polite conversation, and in a lucky thirteenth chapter he begins thus:

I have not yet, Edmund, in teaching you to converse, said anything about poetry; and yet when introduced with judgment into conversation, a verse of poetry is oftentimes very effective. In prose, thoughts are frequently too much spread, while in poetry they are brought more to a point, and affect us more.

Any doubt as to whether this childlike opening may not after all have in it the roots of wisdom is answered when a moment later Edmund is further enlightened by examples:

There is that in a rhyme that catches the attention and clings to the memory. Were I to say, 'Edmund, we must make hay while the sun shines —

> 'Now's the time, and now's the hour,
> By and by the sky may lour ' —

you would see at once that the thing we had in hand was not to be neglected. And if I wanted to cheer your spirits on a dull day, hardly could I do it better than in crying out in a cheerful tone of voice —

> 'Never despair when the fog's in the air;
> A sunshiny morning will come without warning.'

'Oh,' says Edmund with a very natural gaiety, 'I should be in spirits directly.'

'Again' (continues his uncle under this deplorable encouragement), 'you would be likely enough to be impressed with the uncertainty of life were one to say to you in conversation —

> 'Whatever paths our feet may tread,
> Our life is but a spider's thread,

and his sagacity is confirmed by Edmund's delighted: 'I think I should; and hardly could I forget the words.' But the old gentleman's appetite grows by what it feeds on, and before long he reaches triumphant heights.

'You must remember,' he says, 'that the effect of poetry in conversation depends much on the judgment with which it is introduced. Sometimes it is necessary to give a reproof at the moment, and there are instances of this being done with much point and discretion. It is said that Dr. Byrom once reproved an officer for swearing, in the following words —

> Soldier, so tender of thy prince's fame,
> Why make so free with a superior name?
> For thy king's sake the brunt of battle bear,
> But, for the King of kings' sake, never swear.'

'He would not be likely to forget them. They are very striking,' says Edmund with commendable insight, and so the incorrigible old man goes his way.

It all sounds very queer, doubtless. The trick of speech has changed. There is to-day nothing ingenious in the heavy Victorian formality to conceal the emasculation of mind and the absurdity of it all, which are patent enough as we read this little volume of misbegotten humour. As it is set down here the most guileless uncle of to-day would see that there was something amiss in the manner of instruction, and the most unsophisticated Edmund would be suspicious. But the sentiment has lost none of its power. We can very well imagine a popular novelist of to-day saying a good word for an equally popular rhymester something in this way:

The Duke put his hand on the boy's shoulder. Having no son of his own, his nephew was dearer to him than anything in the world, and he never tired in his affectionate admonitions. 'Stick to your games, my boy,' he would often say, 'and always play the game. You must be a manly man. But don't be ashamed of your books. I read a little poetry myself, and often repeat the lines —

> Laugh, and the world laughs with you,
> Weep, and you weep alone,
> For this sad old earth must borrow its mirth,
> But has sorrow enough of its own.'

The boy's mind was already susceptible enough to respond vaguely to the beauty of sentiment in the poet's lines, of which his uncle kept a goodly store in his memory.

It need hardly be said that verse such as 'Laugh, and the world laughs with you,' which makes its appeal by confirming, with an easy trick of rhythm and rhyme, the trite moral reflections with which the minds of its admirers are already well stocked, has no reference to or influence upon the spiritual activity of man. It is not, in any full sense, poetry. It has rhythm, but it has neither excellence of diction nor imaginative intensity. That is to say, the rhythmic impulse is used not to accentuate the imaging of some urgently perceived mood or idea in superbly chosen and ordered words, but merely to gratify a very common habit of mind, the unc-

tuous parading of easy platitudes, by associating
it with an equally common instinct — one which
when expressed passes generally enough for poetry,
but is in itself no more poetry than is a dictionary.
Again, I will not say that those lines about 'the
sad old earth' have never been of any benefit to
anybody. They may have been, just as, I suppose,
somebody or another may have been saved from
indiscretion by remembering that you should look
before you leap, or that you cannot eat your cake
and have it. These proverbial sayings, indeed,
have an attractive flavour, but they do not work
in the way which is poetry's, and still less do the
devices of the didactic rhymester. They may
sometimes regulate a man's discretion, but they
can never penetrate to the roots of his spiritual
being, quickening it with the provocative power
that is art's alone. Born of and communicating
urgent life; that is the nature of poetry, and it is
mere futility to confuse it with the facile rhyming
that comes from borrowed and half-realized
emotion and impresses nothing but a dull inertia
of acceptance. It matters not at all whether the
poet's utterance controls an emotion that has no
apparent strain of moral contemplation, as in:

> 'In Xanadu did Kubla Khan
>   A stately pleasure dome decree:
> Where Alph, the sacred river, ran
> Through caverns measureless to man
>   Down to a sunless sea,'

or one that has so direct and obvious a significance as:

> ' To-morrow, and to-morrow, and to-morrow,
> Creeps in this petty pace from day to day,
> To the last syllable of recorded time;
> And all our yesterdays have lighted fools
> The way to dusty death. Out, out, brief candle!
> Life's but a walking shadow, a poor player
> That struts and frets his hour upon the stage,
> And then is heard no more; it is a tale
> Told by an idiot, full of sound and fury,
> Signifying nothing.'

In either case we are aware, unless we are fundamentally insensible to the challenge of poetry, of a strange and lovely imaginative ardour within us, responding eagerly to the energy from which the poet's word has sprung. And of such ardour, and of such alone, comes all sanity.

A FOOTNOTE TO
'THE SOUL OF MODERN POETRY'

DR. STRACHAN'S name should perhaps be more familiar to us than it is, and his book, 'The Soul of Modern Poetry,' has very little recommendation in the way of a title. And yet it is not only in many ways the most important statement on the subject that has yet been made, but it is difficult to think of any better piece of philosophical criticism since Mr. Bradley's 'Oxford Lectures,' even if one does not have to go further back and name Matthew Arnold. In the midst of much current criticism that is mere dilettante æstheticism, Dr. Strachan's book comes as a refreshment and a challenge. It is a book that is much needed and it should be widely read. Its great value lies in the fact that it approaches poetry again not as a doctrinaire art but as a part of life, of daily life, and as standing or falling ultimately not only by the poets' art but by the moral and philosophic texture out of which that art has sprung. This is not to suggest that Dr. Strachan ever for a moment allows his own personal conclusions to interfere with his judgment of poetry as such. On the contrary, he states clearly and often that any such demand on the part of the world is to destroy the poet who listens to it. But he does forcibly remind a generation that needs it that unless a poet holds opinions about something passionately he can contrive no admirable art. It is not the opinions in themselves that matter, but the passionate holding of them. In experience we know that if they are thus passionately held they are certain of their own virtue. Nothing is idler than the contention that virtuosity sometimes makes, that it is not really quite the thing for a poet to take his own philosophic and moral opinions very seriously.

Of the actual technique and craft of poetry Dr. Strachan has little to say, though the general quality of his book shows that he could speak on these to much purpose if he chose. With certain of his individual judgments, as occasionally with his theory, we are not in agreement. He seems to us to share a common but demonstrable fallacy about Mr. Bernard Shaw. Also, we should dispute his proposition that art has communication as its fundamental intention, or, at least, one of its fundamental intentions, though he is in this with Mr. Lascelles Abercrombie's recent remarkable essay.[1] But these occasional differences do not even qualify our admiration for the book as a whole. In his deductions Dr. Strachan no doubt often knows more than the poets themselves of whom he is writing, but that is the way of good

[1] See *The Poet and Communication.*

constructive criticism. He has a wide and exact
knowledge of contemporary poetry, enforced by
an equal understanding of the great tradition.
There is hardly a page but contains something
memorable. 'No words are used in the same sense
twice' is a phrase well elaborated a little later;
thus:

Words, too, are more than sounds; they are garners
stored with history and the experience of generations
of their users. Languages, also, have their distinctive
characters, and forms of expression and metre suited to
one language do violence to another. Even words seem
to welcome the emotion, the rhythm which the poet
brings, and respond to his touch. This joyous welcome
is the sign of creation. It is poetry.

This is as good for its philosophy as is the following for its human insight:

The most teachable among 'spectators' are not those
who have blithely solved the riddle of this 'unintelli-
gible world,' or have accepted ready-made solutions; but
those who have worn or, however feebly, attempt to
wear their suffering, as men might wear a decoration.

Beside these might be set as a piece of individual
criticism the following of Mr. Thomas Hardy:

One cannot escape the impression that Mr. Hardy
himself is not really unhappy. His is a happiness like
the happiness of the Greek, of which he did not speak
for fear of jealous gods. The delight of Mr. Hardy in
funeral, and those dirges in marriage may, after all, be
but instinctive personations of misery, 'the protective

device,' as Sir Walter Raleigh calls it, of 'a timid happiness.'

Finally, one more passage to show how rich a mind is at work in this book in its general meditation upon life:

The essential nobility of this selflessness, in the interest of Beauty, or Truth, or the Race is not to be denied. To pass for ever out of and beyond one's self is the secret of all great art and, it may be added also, of all great living. 'He that loseth his life shall save it.' Nevertheless, this heroic surrender or rather immolation of personal existence in the interests of a life in general, of a city we shall never see, implies a judgment on the 'worth' of individual life, which marks a distinctly downward progress in our conception of the nature of life. Not only is the general worth of life diminished when we refuse to regard it as in its nature personal, but the character of the omnipotent and all-devouring Divinity whose ends we thus serve is not thereby enhanced. If it is the Race we serve, there is no assurance that even the total life of all the equally fleeting generations of men yet to be, is an end vast enough, or valuable enough, for the sacrifice of even one individual life. Our work will last, and it may be so; but the unbearable tragedy of Death is not that it destroys the work, but that it destroys the worker, not the poem but the poet. The chief tragedy to the modern disbelief in, or sceptical attitude towards immortality is that the poem should be destroyed. This 'god' is inferior to his worshipper, and in character is scarcely to be distinguished from the sovereign God of the ultra-Calvinist, who decreed that a certain number of elect souls should be damned for His own glory and the higher good.

Dr. Strachan is always alert for the 'breath and finer spirit,' and he knows that without it charity and knowledge and good doctrine can never become good poetry. But equally he knows that without conviction the 'breath and finer spirit' itself becomes but a marsh-light signifying nothing. And it is good for poetry and the poets again to be tested by a mind so liberal and so composed.

ANCIENT ALTARS

Still crowned with bays each ancient altar stands

POPE

PHILIP SIDNEY

SIDNEY's reputation as a poet may be said to rest chiefly on his sonnet sequence, 'Astrophel and Stella.' Although in the 'Arcadia' and among the miscellaneous work may be found isolated poems of great beauty, it was when writing 'Astrophel and Stella' that the poet set aside all thought of his ill-considered theories of poetical technique — of which more hereafter — ceased to think of verse-making as a pleasant and polished accomplishment, and wrote with fire and passion as all true poets write, to ease his mind. The few comments which may be offered concerning this his greatest work may be held to apply, broadly speaking, to his less considerable achievements. At the outset, however, it will be well to glance briefly at the state of English poetry at the time when Sidney was writing, and incidentally to clear away such obstacles as his classical experiments which may hinder us in the consideration of his most notable contribution to poetical literature.

We of to-day, looking back on our great line of poets, from Chaucer to Swinburne, find it not a little difficult to adjust our point of view to that of a man born in 1554. Such a one, given the guiding instinct, would see in Chaucer the first and solitary great English poet, succeeded by indifferent imitators, and darkness until the publication of 'Tottel's Miscellany' in 1557. This collection consisted chiefly of the poems of Sir Thomas Wyatt (1503–42) and Henry Howard, Earl of Surrey (1516–47). These poems were remarkable in two ways: for their individual excellence and inspiration, and for the new turn which they gave to the craft of verse-making in England. Of the comparative merits of Wyatt and Surrey, and the respective shares they took in the new movement, it is not necessary to speak here. When they began to write the influence of Chaucer had deteriorated through ill-usage at the hands of many inept disciples, until it had become, for practical purposes, almost negligible. The poet writing to-day, with the accumulated experience and example of half a hundred great names ready to his hand, can scarcely reconstruct the position of the man who feels the impulse to sing, and yet lacks the inspiration and aid of a single great voice before him. The poet, indeed, is no common pick-purse or imitator, yet when he can boast of noble ancestry, his song will of necessity bear in some measure the impress and character of his descent. That this should be so is, of course, both natural and right. Wyatt and Surrey, however, wrote in no such auspicious circumstances. To their own poetical forbears they could look for but little guidance, and they turned to the poets of

Italy and France. From them they borrowed the
sonnet form, which had been popularized in an extraordinary manner by Petrarch, and introduced
it into England. Modifying it in structure and
arrangement, they adhered to certain fundamental
requirements, and in so doing they evolved a certain degree of order out of the chaos into which
English verse had fallen. The chastening influence
of this self-imposed bondage, moreover, brought a
new music and shapeliness into their less regulated
lyrical work. To anything like full understanding
of their craft they did not, of course, attain, but
they left behind them many things of great value
in themselves, and they set up for future and
completer use the framework of a new and great
tradition.

Sidney naturally came under the influence of
these two men, and, partly through them, under
that of their sources, the Italian and French
sonneteers. He was not content, however, to leave
the poetical revolution exactly where he had found
it, and with Spencer, his senior by two years, and
Gabriel Harvey, he conceived the idea of introducing classical metres into English verse. He, too,
realized that some reform was called for, and considered that no better method could be adopted
than that employed in the masterpieces of the
ancients. The result was a woeful proof of the
futility of attempting to impose the manner and

possibilities of one language on another. That the experiment was an unqualified failure is no matter for wonder; that two such men as Spenser and Sidney should have discussed it seriously, is. Fortunately Spenser learnt to laugh at the whole question, and Sidney to discount it by his practice.

The point need not be carried further. There is, however, another aspect of this question of foreign influence which is of the utmost importance. Sidney — and this consideration applies to the whole group of Elizabethan sonneteers — in going to foreign models for guidance in the matter of form, carried away with him not a little of their substance. Modern scholarship has shown these predatory excursions to have been both frequent and considerable in extent. It has, in a way, proved its case up to the hilt, by advancing numberless instances where an image or whole phrase has been appropriated without a qualm. In some cases, indeed, a complete sonnet is little more than a fairly close translation, and Thomas Watson, at least, admitted openly that his sequence of irregular stanzas, 'The Tears of Fancy,' was no more than this. In Sidney's case, however, as in that of most of his contemporaries, the work is set before us as being original, and a decision as to whether this claim is or is not to be allowed, is obviously of great moment. 'Astrophel and Stella' being a love poem, the first thing to be done when it is submitted to

our judgment is to enquire whether it be sincere.
The writers who have so convincingly denoted the
debt of the Elizabethans to foreign models in form
and stray — or even numerous — expressions and
images, have directed us into an interesting field
of poetical history. When, however, from these
ascertained facts they proceed to draw deductions
which set aside all the claims which the poet makes
as being most essential to his function, dissent becomes imperative. We are told that these sonnets
are no more than a clever exercise, displaying here
and there a pretty fancy and a delicate ear for a
musical phrase, having for their substance hearsay
and conventional attitudes, devoid of all inventive-
ness, passion, and conviction. That they are, in
short, written precisely as poetry should not be
written, from the head and not from the heart.
At this stage of the enquiry we come to something
beyond the application of judicial learning to facts,
we come to the application of our feeling to that of
the poet.

> 'When my good angel guides me to the place
> Where all my good I do in Stella see,
> That heav'n of joys throws only down on me
> Thund'ring disdains and lightnings of disgrace;
> But when the rugged'st step of Fortune's race
> Makes me fall from her sight, then sweetly she
> With words wherein the Muses' treasures be,
> Shows love and pity to my absent case.
> Now I, wit-beaten long by hardest fate,
> So dull am, that I cannot look into

> The ground of this fierce love and lovely hate.
> Then, some good body, tell me how I do,
> Whose presence absence, absence presence is;
> Blest in my curse, and cursed in my bliss.'

If writing like that is artificial, it is an artificiality the secret of which has been lost, for utterance of the kind only rises to-day from the deep wells of emotion.

In this connection there is, however, a special circumstance in Sidney's case to be considered. The Stella of the sonnets was Penelope Devereux, daughter of the Earl of Essex. So much is clear from both external and internal evidence. The known facts of her history, in so far as it affects her relations with Sidney, may be told briefly. They met when he was just over twenty years of age, she barely thirteen. Shortly afterwards there was talk of a match, favoured by the parents on both sides, concerning which the parties chiefly interested were naturally — in view of the girl's age — not of any decided opinions. For no clearly assigned reason the matter fell through, though for the next four or five years it was still under consideration. It is clear that at this time neither he nor she entertained any serious affection for the other. In 1581, at the age of eighteen, Penelope married Lord Rich, from whom she was ultimately divorced to become the wife of the Earl of Devonshire, after having been that nobleman's

mistress for some years. That her first marriage
was unhappy is evident, and the conclusions drawn
from these scanty premises are usually somewhat
as follows:

Sidney, we are told, really loved Penelope from
the first, but, being in no hurry to marry, let year
after year go by without taking definite steps.
Further, distracted by his court and official duties
and his interests at Penshurst and Wilton, he was
less ardent in his wooing than the lady desired.
At length, partly out of pique, partly out of des-
peration, she married Lord Rich, and this event
came to her old lover in the nature of a catastrophe. That which he could long since have had
for the taking was now beyond his reach, and his
desire was quickened and increased tenfold. His
pent-up passion at length broke from its silence,
and poured itself out in song. Then come new
critics and very justly observe that all this is im-
probable in the extreme. That we know enough of
Sidney's character not to believe that had he truly
loved Penelope he would have dallied and made a
fool both of himelf and her. That he was a man of
singularly clear judgment and self-knowledge, and
that had his will been to marry this girl he would
have given it effect. In demolishing one indefensible position, however, they proceed, I think, to set
themselves up in another. Sidney did not, as is
shown by the facts, they say, bear any sincere

devotion to Penelope. Nevertheless this same Penelope is the object of the passionate declarations of the sonnets, and, therefore, the sonnets themselves are insincere, and become merely the ingenious display of a considerable poetic talent. In order effectively to cut off our retreat in all directions, they urge that if by any means the sonnets can be shown to be sincere, then they are certainly shown to be immoral, inasmuch as the object of these amorous protestations was a married woman. And so we have this elusive question of a poet's creativeness reduced to the most matter-of-fact rule-of-thumb that could be desired.

It may be granted at once that scattered through the sonnets are many signs of the poet's debt to his sources in more than actual structure; that an idea is not infrequently taken from Petrarch or his followers. Further, that superficially they bear indisputable evidence of having been written for Lady Rich, the historical personage of whom we have a more or less complete record; and lastly, that they are adorned or marred throughout by the conceits and extravagances which were the poetic fashion of the age. Then let us read the sequence carefully, and undisturbed by the hundred jarring theories as to its biographical interpretation, and we shall, I think, come to a decision which it is inconceivable could have at any time been overlooked. Poetic truth is a greater thing than the truth of courts and schools, and the sign of poetic truth is written large over the pages of 'Astrophel and Stella.' A poet does not make a pretence of purging his soul for the entertainment of his fellows, nor does he use his poetry as a catalogue wherein to record the facts of his life. Sidney was in love. With whom is a question that does not concern us in the least; in all probability — it is indeed probable to the point of certainty — it was with none but an ideal of his own. As a framework upon which to build his ideal he chose Penelope Rich, and so the ideal became invested with certain of the qualities and circumstances of the material woman.

To suppose that the object of a poet's love and worship is either a definite being possessed of certain known attributes, or else a mere unsubstantial unreality from which he can gather no inspiration and support, is utterly to misunderstand both the poet and his poetry. It is a common thing to laugh lightly at the idea of a man being in love with love. The state is generally regarded as being incidental to nonage, a youthful abnormality that will burn itself out rapidly and finally. The truth is that many men and all poets are in love with love till the end of their days. The poet may be united to one woman and faithful to her, or he may from time to time fall under the spell of many, but, however this may be, he will create for his inmost need an ideal transcending his earthly love, fashioned indeed out of the material and suggestion of this love, but wrought into perfection on the anvil of his own imagination. Shelley we know wove 'Epipsychidion' out of his acquaintance with Emilia Viviani, but Mary Shelley was wise enough to understand that the poem was the poet's creation. Tennyson wrote 'In Memoriam,' and therein made Hallam a more supreme type of the friend than any man could ever be of himself; and was the Beatrice of Dante's song the daughter of a Florentine citizen? These reflections do not, of course, detract one whit from the honour and power of womanhood, but they do remind us of the danger and folly of attempting to reduce the poet's creation to the proportions of biographical fact. The material that a woman brings the poet upon which to build may be great or small; in Sidney's case it was probably slight, but it was sufficient for his purpose. Out of it he wrought a glowing passion of song, which may be hopelessly bewildering if we attempt to read it in the light of dates and records, but which becomes gracious and clear if we pass it through the fire of the imagination.

I do not for a moment suggest that this idealization by the poet of his love determines the existence of the physical side of his passion; on the other hand, the imaginative love of the poet is complete in every way. It is quite possible that some

of the incidents of 'Astrophel and Stella' referred to
particular occurrences — for example, the meeting
described in the fourth song. The important point
to bear in mind is that the essential truth of these
things is not in the least affected by the consideration as to whether they had or had not their counterpart in actual physical occurrences. Love is
both of the flesh and of the spirit, and such is the
love of which Sidney sings from a full store of
imaginative experience. It is not for us to demand
that this experience shall coincide with his diary.

'Astrophel and Stella' was first published by
Thomas Newman, without authority, in 1591, that
is to say five years after Sidney's death. It is clear
from the Preface that the poems had long been in
circulation in manuscript, but there is nothing to
show that the poet himself had ever prepared them
in any way for the press. In view of this circumstance their freedom from obscurities is remarkable, no less than their singular smoothness and
polish. It must be remembered that no poet of
magnitude had arisen between Surrey and Sidney,
and the technical advance beyond 'Tottel's Miscellany' is enormous. It is possible, perhaps, that
Sidney had seen some of Spenser's sonnets which
were to be published in 1595 under the title of
'Amoretti' but, even so, they would not be sufficiently in perspective at the time to exercise any
profound influence, however apparent their beauty

might be. And, moreover, Sidney need not fear comparison with any other Elizabethan sonnet-eer save Shakespeare. The epithet 'sugared,' so commonly applied by critics of those days to contemporary poetry, has with us fallen into discredit as implying superfluous ornament and mere prettiness. When it was used it meant, precisely, sweet, and it was applied to Sidney's verse with perfect justice. In the whole sequence it would be difficult to pick out a score of halting lines, and this, when we remember the state in which the poet found English versification, is extraordinary. The sonnet form as he uses it is a compromise between the pure Italian type and the English type, as used and made finally distinctive by Shakespeare. In the octave he generally adopts the Petrarchan rhyme scheme *a b b a a b b a*, with the occasional variation — *a b a b a b a b*. He never departs from the rule that the octave shall contain but two rhymes. In the sextet he is less regular, in most instances making use of the final couplet, and allowing himself any sequence for his three rhymes. Thus he observes the Italian arrangement of the octave and limitation to five rhymes in all, but generally infringes the rule of the sextet. It is not without interest to trace the descent of the sonnet from Petrarch to Shakespeare in this manner, using as illustration the type most generally used in each case:

Petrarch................	*a b b a*	*a b b a*	*c d e c d e* `
Sidney.................	*a b b a*	*a b b a*	*c d c d e e* or *c c d e e d*
Spenser.................	*a b a b*	*b c b c*	*c d c d e e*
Shakespeare.............	*a b a b*	*c d c d*	*e f e f g g*

A great deal of critical discussion has arisen as to the æsthetic value of these varying forms. What appears to be the root intention of the sonnet, namely, that the close of the octave should carry the tide of feeling and expression to its highest and most commanding point, and that this should find a more or less subdued lapse in the sextet, was of course defeated by the Elizabethan use of the final couplet, which serves rather to emphasize than repress the last note. In similar manner the latitude allowed in the number of rhymes in the English sonnet operates against that unity and conciseness which is properly characteristic of the form. It must be allowed that, all things considered, the Petrarchan type, with its rigid exclusion of all diffuseness, its recurrent beat, and its subtle arrangement of the sextet, whereby the rhymes are so placed as to avoid too great a sweetness and yet are just evident enough to satisfy the ear, is best fitted to lend the sonnet that dignity and lofty economy of expression which place it in poetry as a thing apart. At the same time dogmatism here, as in all things critical, is speedily confronted with its own folly. Mr. Harold H. Child, in touching upon one of the points above mentioned, sums up the whole question in a single observation:

'But the final couplet,' he says, 'has been used so freely and to such noble ends by English writers that objection is out of place.' [1]

The same may, of course, be said of all the variations and licenses to which I have alluded.

The only other observation to be made in the matter of the prosody of 'Astrophel and Stella' is that Sidney in a few instances uses lines of twelve syllables instead of the orthodox ten. This is a transgression which it is not so easy to defend; indeed, it is, I think, indefensible. The ten-syllable line is as essential to the character of the English sonnet as it is to that of English blank verse, and it may well be said that on this point if no other the requirement of the form admits no denial. One has only to look at an example of trespass in this direction, say the eighth sonnet of 'Astrophel and Stella,' to perceive the extraordinary effect of incongruity that is produced. The lilting jog-trot of the line is agreeable enough in itself, but as we read on and find it wedded to a singularly austere rhyme arrangement, we feel as we should do if Mercutio spoke with the voice of Hamlet.

Sidney's vocabulary was both extensive and flexible. He had in a marked degree the faculty of investing a familiar word with a deepened signifi-

[1] *Cambridge History of English Literature*, vol. III, chap. VIII.

cance, rather than use a strange or eccentric one. The opening of one of the most famous sonnets in the series will suffice to illustrate this:

> 'With how sad steps, O Moon, thou climb'st the skies.
> How silently, and with how wan a face!
> What, may it be that even in heav'nly place
> That busy archer his sharp arrows tries?'

It will be observed that there is no word here which is in the least uncommon, and yet by their disposition and through the conviction and feeling behind them they take on a distinctive atmosphere and become poetical in the true sense of the term. This power is, of course, one of the greatest that an artist can possess, and Sidney possessed it in full measure. In point of imagery he is not so decidedly successful. He was in no way free from the prevailing vice of conceit-making, and he too frequently seeks to illustrate his statement by mere fanciful decoration instead of penetrating imaginative parallel. What he has to say he says generally clearly and in suggestive, well-chosen language, but he seldom drives his utterance home by any elaboration which he may make. To do this, however, except on the rarest occasions, is an achievement reserved for the greatest alone, and by the greatest is implied the few who are great at all points, and it is no discredit to Sidney to say that he was not of these; he may still take rank with immortal names.

A poet to whom excellence can be allowed only on comparative and circumstantial grounds is, after all, in poor case. If he is only good as a pioneer, or for his years, or for his station, he cannot rightly be said to be good at all. As a pioneer Sidney makes an unanswerable claim to praise. He stands shoulder to shoulder with Spenser in the great movement of English verse. His friend, indeed, attained heights which he did not attempt, but he shares with him the honour of introducing new light and grace and strength into the verse that had already been beaten into some comeliness by the poets of 'Tottel's Miscellany.' His claims do not, however, end here. Apart from all relative considerations, and judged solely as a poet by the highest standards which we can find, he occupies an honourable place in our literature. His poems are worthy to be read, and are read, to-day for their positive achievement. Taking up a vehicle which was at the time experimental and lacking in any finality of polish, he imparted to it a sweetness which at its best has rarely been excelled, and he used it to give expression to griefs and exultations of his own experience.

JOHN MILTON

JOHN MILTON, by common consent of critical opinion, holds a place among the first three great English poets. This is not to say that there are not a dozen, or even twenty, writers in the succession of English poetry who at times in individual quality touch a height equal to Milton's own. The word 'great' is one that is commonly used about poets, often too easily, and generally, I suppose, with a difference. What is meant at the moment is that Milton stands preëminently for a very important kind of achievement in poetry, and, so far as can be seen in perspective up to our own day, there are hardly more than two other poets of whom the same thing can so definitely be said. There were many poets among the Elizabethans who in their best moments had as clearly the stuff of poetry in them as Shakespeare himself, but in breadth and consistency of performance Shakespeare transcends them all. It may be said that there is nothing which they did that he did not do as well and generally better. He was the chief and crowning glory of a vast range of poetic activity, practised by many men of great endowments, and, profiting as he did by their efforts and example, he brought the whole movement to its most perfect expression. So that, both by his personal quality and the actual volume of his work, it is of Shakespeare that we think instinctively as *the* great poet of his time. Because his time happened to be one of peculiar virtue as an inspiration to poetry, a time when the nation, both in adventure and culture, was first becoming delightedly aware of its own splendour and vitality, and was content to enjoy the spectacle of life, and share in its ardours purely for their own invigorating sake, without reducing them to moral or social problems, he comes to our minds always, perhaps, as the greatest poet of all. After him there are two other poets in the English story of whom something of the same kind may be said, John Milton and William Wordsworth. Circumstances of history made it impossible for either of these to inform their work with quite the same happy ease of spiritual youth that marks even the tragedies of Shakespeare, but each in his own way preëminently stood for one of the great natural movements in English poetry. After Wordsworth there is no poet of whom we can yet be quite sure in this matter. There are many whose work is certain of individual fame for ever, but none of whom we can yet say that he, above all others, most clearly embodied that strange urge in one direction which underlies all the manifold workings of an epoch.

John Milton's claim to greatness by this standard rests, to put it very briefly, on his unwearying desire, implicit through all his work and once plainly confessed, to 'justify the ways of God to men.' The whole Puritan revolutionary movement in England was something more than a protest against the evil doing of Charles the First. That was the occasion of its immediate expression in arms, but behind it all there was something far more constructive than this indignation, splendid though that was. The Elizabethan age — the accepted definition is as good as another — had been one of immense unquestioning activity. Physical adventure, the crossing of great seas in small boats, a childlike gaiety of response to the colour and arrogance of Renaissance culture that poured into the mind of the country from Italy, it was all a very festival of ardent and powerful youth. That, we know, is not the complete story, or, rather, a story with no need of qualification. Squalor and pedantry and mincing logic were not unknown, but these were accidental to, and not characteristic of, the time, which remained essentially one of eager and unquestioning joy in life, a finely irresponsible joy it may almost be said. When this impulse had spent itself, and the magnificence of youth had passed, there followed a time when the conscience of the nation became a deliberate thing, setting itself to assess the ardours of a day now gone. It was this spirit of argued judgment as distinguished from simple and delighted acceptance, that was at the very roots of the whole Puritan revolution in England. It was not necessarily an angry judgment nor a self-righteous one, nor even a grudging one, but it was judgment, and its high priest was John Milton.

The outline of Milton's life may be told in a few words. The son of a middle-class family, he was born in London in 1608, was educated at Saint Paul's School and Christ's College, Cambridge, where he graduated in 1629, wrote most of his shorter poems, including 'L'Allegro' and 'Il Penseroso,' 'Comus,' and 'Lycidas,' before he was thirty, went on the Continental Tour, and at the age of thirty-two, having become the tutor of his nephews, he seemed to have forsaken poetry for political and social pamphleteering. He signalized his marriage to Mary Powell in 1643 by a pamphlet — not, it may be said, without very considerable provocation — on 'The Doctrine and Discipline of Divorce' which was followed by 'Areopagitica' in 1644. In 1649, after the execution of the King, he was made Latin Secretary to the Council of State, and continued his controversial writing with 'Eikonoklastes,' a reply to the King's book, and other essays which contain some of the finest and most vehement, if not best-tempered, prose in the language. His blindness began in 1651, and among his secretarial assistants was the poet Andrew Marvell. Losing his official position at the Restoration, he was for a time in hiding. He married for a second time in 1656, and again a third in 1662. His remaining years were spent partly at Chalfont Saint Giles and partly in London; he died at the age of sixty-six in 1674, and was buried in Saint Giles's, Cripplegate.

In 1645 he had collected his smaller poems for publication, and a second edition of the volume was issued with additions in 1673. His great works were published, 'Paradise Lost' in 1667, and 'Paradise Regained' and 'Samson Agonistes' in 1671. He is supposed to have begun writing the first of these as early as 1650, and the story of his dictating his masterpieces to his daughters is well known. His long silence as a poet in the middle of his life is difficult to explain, preoccupied though he may have been with political matters. We may, however, be sure that during the years when he was not actively writing poetry he was meditating the great work in front of him and preparing himself for a task as to the responsibility of which he was very deliberately conscious. His muse was to address itself to 'Things unattempted yet in prose or rhyme.' And, as he tells us, in his 'Apology for Smectymnuus' (1641), he believed that 'He who would not be frustrate of his hope to write well hereafter in laudable things ought himself to be a true poem.'

He came to the composition of the great works

of his later years a good scholar, the chief intellectual champion in his country of political and religious freedom, and a man deeply versed in the sorrows and disillusions of life. In taking for his themes the fall of Satan, the redemption of the world by the Son of Man, and the sufferings of Samson, he was following the example of the Greeks in choosing stories which should be familiar to his readers. The mere invention of a fable as an exercise for his genius appealed to him no more than it did to Shakespeare, and he preferred to lavish the vast stores of his energy upon the spiritual and imaginative significance with which the mould of accepted fables could be filled. The literature which has grown up round these poems in itself forms a library of theology, poetics, and philosophy.

To attempt anything like an analysis of the vast subject-matter of Milton's writings is here obviously impossible. Of the poetry itself it may at once be said that it cannot be approached profitably in any light or easy mood. Once to have come under the spell of the serene mastery of Milton's genius is to be made free of it for ever. It is impossible once to like Milton's poetry and then to grow tired of it, but it may well sometimes be that a reader who is happy enough with some tripping or homely muse should find the ceremony of the great Puritan a little difficult, though 'L'Allegro' and 'Il Penseroso,' together with passages from

'Comus' and 'Lycidas,' can hardly fail to be pleasing to anybody. But for the rest of us there comes a time when the full glory of Milton's last period is a thing in life as inevitable in its authority as the beauty of nature itself. Matthew Arnold's 'Others abide our question, thou art free,' is as true of the other supreme poets as it is of Shakespeare. If we have the love of English poetry in our blood at all, we can no longer argue about:

> 'Of Man's first disobedience and the fruit
> Of that forbidden tree, whose mortal taste
> Brought death into the world and all our woe,
> With loss of Eden, till one greater Man
> Restore us and regain the blissful seat,
> Sing heav'nly Muse, that on the secret top
> Of Oreb, or of Sinai, didst inspire
> That shepherd, who first taught the chosen seed,
> In the beginning how the heav'ns and earth
> Rose out of Chaos; or if Sion hill
> Delight thee more, and Siloa's brook that flow'd
> Fast by the oracle of God; I thence
> Invoke thy aid to my advent'rous song,
> That with no middle flight intends to soar
> Above th' Aonian mount, while it pursues
> Things unattempted yet in prose or rhyme.
>   And chiefly thou, O Spirit, that dost prefer
> Before all temples th' upright heart and pure,
> Instruct me, for thou know'st; thou from the first
> Wast present, and with mighty wings outspread
> Dove-like sat'st brooding on the vast abyss,
> And mad'st it pregnant: what in me is dark
> Illumine, what is low raise and support;
> That to the height of this great argument
> I may assert eternal Providence,
> And justify the ways of God to men.'

This spiritual exaltation Milton in his later works maintained, with hardly a break, for something like fifteen thousand lines. In doing it he achieved a style which in its union of opulence and severity was at the time, and has remained, without parallel. As always with the great men, the poetry transcends the argument. The argument was indeed a passionate enough conviction with Milton himself, and was the foundation from which the mighty edifice of his poetry rose. But it is the poetry itself that, in the right mood, is a defence against the ignominies of the world as hardly any other English poetry is. Milton did very ardently wish to 'justify the ways of God to men,' to scourge tyranny, and to exalt the undying heroism of man. But in these things he was but one of many thousand generous spirits who have passed on earth, and his testament was made in terms of a mythology and a political temper which in themselves are not very intimately stirring things to us to-day. But, unlike those other thousands, Milton was a great poet, and, as such, he both transcended for ever the conditions of the moment and lifted his personal passion into universal poise by the sublime certainty with which it was embodied. Poise — that is the last word when all critical analysis of Milton has been made. To read 'Paradise Lost' or 'Samson Agonistes,' without haste and without question, is to look upon the troubled

world with untroubled eyes. The purging is not
of the same kind as that effected by the great poets
of the tragic human emotions, where the salvation
is wrought by the spectator being moved to a God-
like compassion for suffering or erring man. Reading one of the great Shakespeare tragedies we are
so touched to pity that we not only feel that in the
course of justice there ought to be some final compensation for the disaster which we have witnessed,
but that in some strange way we have been given
the power to will that it shall be so. Milton, even in
'Samson Agonistes,' where the actual fable is one of
human catastrophe, does not move us in quite the
same way. Here we feel not so much as we do in
Shakespeare's tragedies that when all has been
endured mercy will come, as it were, from some
common impulse of the world to heal even the most
merited suffering, but that the spirit of man can
mysteriously rise clear of its own limitations and
that man is, in fact, greater than the expression
that he can ever give to himself in the conduct of
life. Shakespeare's way is the more human, the
more passionate, and the more intimately related
to our common moods, but there are times when
Milton can bring us a reassurance that is altogether
his own.

The keen spiritual light that is over all Milton's
meditation does not lessen the warmth of his humanity, a quality we are apt to forget was his when

we think of him. His early poems, though they are
marked already by the ceremony that in the great
works was to come to such grandeur of style, are
the work of a young poet moving freely about the
world, generous and even gay in temper. Whatever
his austerity of manner, there was no coldness at
the heart of the man who could write:

> 'While the ploughman near at hand
> Whistles o'er the furrow'd land,
> And the milkmaid singeth blithe,
> And the mower whets his scythe,
> And every shepherd tells his tale
> Under the hawthorn in the dale. . . .'

Nor, when 'Paradise Lost' appeared more than
twenty years later, had the note gone:

> 'So hand in hand they pass'd, the loveliest pair
> That ever since in love's embraces met;
> Adam the goodliest man of men since born
> His sons, the fairest of her daughters Eve.
> Under a tuft of shade, that on a green
> Stood whisp'ring soft, by a fresh fountain side
> They sat them down; and after no more toil
> Of their sweet gard'ning labour than sufficed
> To recommend cool Zephyr, and made ease
> More easy, wholesome thirst and appetite
> More grateful, to their supper fruits they fell. . . .'

a passage the tenderness of which is recurrent
throughout the poem whenever Milton's thought
for a moment leaves the height of its great argument and dwells on the human joys and sorrows
of Paradise. While, however, he is thus always

able to remind us of his command of the gentler things of holiday and pathos, it remains the truth that it is in a sublime philosophic conception of life, rather than in the particular and intimate lives of men and women, that his interest chiefly lies and in the expression of which his mastery is most commonly used.

> 'How soon hath Time, the subtle thief of youth,
>> Stol'n on his wing my three and twentieth year!
>> My hasting days fly on with full career,
> But my late spring no bud or blossom show'th.
> Perhaps my semblance might deceive the truth,
>> That I to manhood am arrived so near,
>> And inward ripeness doth much less appear,
>> That some more timely-happy spirits indu'th.
> Yet be it less or more, or soon or slow,
>> It shall be still in strictest measure even
>> To that same lot, however mean or high,
> Toward which Time leads me, and the will of Heaven.
>> All is, if I have grace to use it so,
>> As ever in my great Task-master's eye.'

There at twenty-three was already the promise of the poet who in the full maturity of his power was to learn how, by pure majesty of spirit and the very magic of verse, to bring even angels into the range of our human sympathies, as in:

> 'So spake the seraph Abdiel faithful found,
> Among the faithless, faithful only he:
> Among innumerable false unmoved,
> Unshaken, unseduced, unterrified,
> His loyalty he kept, his love, his zeal;
> Nor number, nor example with him wrought
> To swerve from truth, or change his constant mind
> Though single. . . .'

and who when he brought these faculties to a life still generalized, but nearer to our own experience, as at the end of 'Samson Agonistes,' could achieve a moving beauty which has never been excelled in English poetry:

> 'Nothing is here for tears, nothing to wail
> Or knock the breast, no weakness, no contempt,
> Dispraise, or blame, nothing but well and fair,
> And what may quiet us in a death so noble. . . .'

Although, more perhaps than most poets, Milton allowed a life of affairs to encroach upon his actual poetical composition, there is no poet of whom it can be more justly said that he devoted his life to poetry. Having proved his gifts in the early poems, he determined to wait until such time as he felt himself to be equipped for a work that should not only be profound in conception but massive in volume and architecture. 'Neither do I think it shame,' he writes in the 'Reason of Church Government urged against Prelatry' of 1641, 'to covenant with any knowing reader that, for some years yet I may go on trust with him toward the payment of what I am now indebted, as being a work not to be raised from the heat of youth or the vapours of wine . . . but by devout prayer to that eternal Spirit, who can enrich with all utterance and knowledge . . . to this must be added industrious and select reading, steady observation, insight into all seemly and generous art and affairs. . . .' Through those years of political and religious controversy his mind was fixed constantly upon the redemption of this promise. The result of all this was that when the works came they were upon a scale that can be no more lightly apprehended by the reader than they were lightly conceived by the poet. Before we can come to anything like the full significance of Milton's great poems we must read them steadily and we must read them whole.

We may for purposes of argument do very well in dividing poets up into schools, Classical, Romantic, Realist, and so forth, but when we come to the very great men we find that in some measure or another they have the best qualities of all these different kinds. Nowhere has the case for the so-called Classic as against the Romantic method been put more lucidly, than in Matthew Arnold's famous 'Preface' of 1853:

We can hardly at the present day understand what Menander meant, when he told a man who enquired as to the progress of his comedy that he had finished it, not having yet written a single line, because he had constructed the action of it in his mind. A modern critic would have assured him that the merit of his piece depended on the brilliant things which arose under his pen as he went along. We have poems which seem to exist merely for the sake of single lines and passages; not for the sake of producing any total-impression. We have critics who seem to direct their attention merely to detached expressions, to the language about the action, not to the action itself. I verily think that the majority of them do not in their hearts believe that there is such a thing as a total-impression to be derived from a poem at all, or to be demanded from a poet; they think the term a commonplace of metaphysical criticism. They will permit the Poet to select any action he pleases, and to suffer that action to go as it will, provided he gratifies them with occasional bursts of fine writing, and with a shower of isolated thoughts and images. That is, they permit him to leave their poetical sense ungratified, provided that he gratifies their rhetorical sense and their curiosity.

This is an admirable piece of æsthetic theory and it was a point that very much needed to be made, and for that matter still needs to be made to-day in view of the common practice of modern poetry. But the argument is one which when we come to the poets themselves in their poetry — even to Matthew Arnold in his own poetry — we find to need qualification. It is true that certain poets, chiefly lyric poets, do make good their claim to our remembrance almost entirely because of the occasional verbal felicities of which Arnold speaks, and they do not achieve, or, perhaps, even aim at, that 'total-impression' which the critic so rightly holds up to admiration. But this does not mean that the poets who are masters of proportion and form on the grand scale are indifferent to the appeal of those same verbal felicities. How, for example, would Arnold account for Keats in his reckoning? The form of the 'Odes,' although it is of small dimensions, has decided grandeur and the 'total-impression' is emphatic and lasting. And yet Keats took the greatest pains to 'load every rift with ore.' There is hardly a line without some exquisite touch of the kind that Arnold, in his enthusiasm for classic purity, seems almost to censure. As I have pointed out, no poetry could be more suggestive in this matter than Arnold's own, where the general effect is always kept in view with scrupulous loyalty to the poet's belief, but where 'showers of isolated thoughts and images' are constantly breaking upon the design to our great profit.

In Milton this richness of phrase, beautiful even apart from its context, is constant. 'The tann'd haycock in the mead,' 'The glowing violet,' 'Brisk as the April buds in Primrose season,' 'Beauty is Nature's brag,' 'They also serve who only stand and wait,' 'The marble air,' 'And from sweet kernals prest She tempers dulcet creams,' 'And calm of mind all passion spent —' such things come to the eye on almost any page. Great and essential as the complete design is, it is not difficult ever to make Milton's inspiration clear by short passages, even phrases. But the design remains, to be discovered only by the patient and humble reader. Once to behold it, in all its lordly power and grace, is to rejoice in one of the sublime achievements of English character and of English poetry.

THOMAS GRAY

THE acute power of observation that Alexander Pope applied so admirably to the manners of his time and the foibles of humanity was not wholly set aside in his contemplation of man's spiritual life and the beauty of the natural world. A tradition, not false in itself, but false in him because he accepted it without a poet's conviction, was, indeed, continually set between him and the thing seen. He could not see a woodland without pretending to himself that he also saw it peopled by 'coy nymphs,' and a flock of sheep outraged his sense of decency unless it was accompanied by Pan. But, in spite of this imaginative trickery, he had moments when he came near to seeing the loveliness of earth with undistracted vision, and they are moments that afford a striking commentary on the essential weakness of his poetry and that of his age. Whilst it is true that the sublime is but a step from the ridiculous, it is equally true that the greatest poets, those who have most often encompassed the sublime, are also those who have had least fear of the false step that should lead them to disaster. They have not infrequently taken it, and been utterly unashamed, probably not even conscious of their lapse. Great poetry is never self-conscious; however carefully it may be wrought, the care is a concession to the poet's desire to express fully the thing that he has discovered, and not to his sense of propriety. The profoundest imaginative truth in poetry is often embodied in an utterance quite unable to bear examination by common standards of fact. A level-headed lawyer, who carried truth in a nutshell, reading Shelley's 'Skylark,' came to the phrase 'Thou scorner of the ground.' 'Nonsense,' he exclaimed, 'the bird makes its nest on the ground.' The besetting sin of the temper in poetry for which Pope stood was precisely this self-consciousness, this distrust of poetic truth, this fear of the ridiculous. So that Pope, looking out on to distant hills and seeing that they were blue, was troubled. He knew that they were really green or brown, in any case not blue. And then he began to doubt whether even in appearance they were quite blue after all, and finally suppressed the poet that was in him and wrote:

'There wrapt in clouds the *blueish* hills ascend.'

Propriety was unoffended, and we were given an epitome in one line of the twist that did so much to devitalize the poetry of the age.

As if to emphasize the essential unity of matter and manner in art, this timorousness of spirit found its exact parallel in the form into which poetry was shaped. The prevalence of the heroic couplet cannot have been due to any conviction in the minds of the poets that this was indisputably the form best fitted for the language. But it was capable of a balance, a regularity, a precision that commended it with peculiar force to men to whom these things were of first-rate importance in their reading of life. Once it had been handled by a master technician, it was thenceforth easy to determine at a glance whether the versification was correct, and the appeal to correctness was sacrosanct. Any departure from recognized rules could be instantly detected: a most comfortable privilege to men who valued rule more than adventure. Rejecting blank verse as sorting ill with that elegance which was a plaything for polite society, the poets were not disposed to surrender those qualities of blank verse most suited to their formal habit of mind. The five foot line was established as the staple of English verse, and by stripping it of variety and lending it the adornment of rhyme they found a vehicle as rigid as their own perceptions and at the same time not devoid of authority. To have experimented with more flexible lyrical forms would have been, in their eyes, wilful folly, for flexibility meant a confusion of standards, a license that would have destroyed the simple code of reference to which they were used. The relationship of early eighteenth-century poetry in England to classicism is extremely remote. In great classic art, as in great art of every kind, the supreme arbiter is the imagination, and it was the radical flaw of that phase of English poetry that the imagination was subjected not merely to the reason, but to a reason that continually argued back to formal standards and not forward to discoveries. The poets were not even progressive in their science.[1]

To praise a poet because he achieved in spite of great difficulties rather than for his achievement itself is to serve him ill. The external circumstance of John Clare's poverty adds nothing to the worth of his lyrics. We may be astonished at the spectacle of a penniless and untutored labourer adding to the store of authentic poetry, but our astonishment has nothing to do with our understanding of art. It is not our concern, in seeking for the beauty that is the gift of art, to remember that Milton was blind or Beethoven deaf. We may acclaim Chaucer because he shaped a language, but we love him because he was a poet, and it is by our love that he is immortal. It is the function of poetry to impart to us strong exaltation, to free our imaginations and quicken our spiritual perceptions, and if it fails to do this no plea of disabilities or obstacles will serve the poet. That he might have done better under other circumstances, or that he did well con-

---

[1] This by way of suggesting the limitations that Gray broke through. For a note on the more significant qualities of the earlier eighteenth-century poetry see the paper on Wordsworth.

sidering this thing or that, does not matter. The poet's revelation alone can move us, and his written word is the only revelation that we can accept. If he fails to reveal we may still be interested in the failure, but for reasons remote from the divine curiosity that leads us to poetry.

There are, however, circumstances that, whilst not increasing the positive value of a poet's work, may throw his achievement into greater relief. Thomas Gray, who was born when Pope was twenty-eight years old, holds his place among the poets because he had something to reveal, and with whatever uncertainty and in however small a compass, found fit expression for the thing that he had to say, and for no other reason. But he arrests particular attention in the course of English poetry because he was the first man of importance to revolt against the formalism of the poets of the age into which he was born. The distinction was shared by Collins, who heralded the great romantic revival with a note of purer poetry than that of the poet who is more widely known, but the two men were working independently to the same end. Gray certainly owed nothing to Collins; he might, indeed, have done so with gain. His judgment was not at any time as sound in this matter of contemporary poetry as his instinct. He worked away from the things that he praised and towards the things in which he professed to see no virtue. We find him

speaking highly of Shenstone and Beattie and
Mason, and yet writing to his friend Wharton,
'Have you seen the works of two young authors, a
Mr. Warton and Mr. Collins, both writers of odes?
it is odd enough, but each is the half of a considerable man, and one the counterpart of the other.
The first has but little invention, very poetical
choice of expression, and a good ear. The second,
a fine fancy, modelled upon the antique, a bad ear,
great variety of words and images, with no choice
at all. They both deserve to last some years, but
will not.' But the denial of the false tradition by
which he was surrounded was no less emphatic
because it was more or less unconscious. Gray's
habitual outlook upon the world was rather of the
scholarly observer than that of the creative seer,
but he had moments of genuinely imaginative
vision, and his instinct impelled him to allow these
free and not unadventurous expression. Lyrical
verse during the hundred years that followed him
attained a variety and colour that would have
seemed even to his independent mind the merest
vagary and licentiousness; but in his rather for-
mally constructed odes, and even in the simple
stanzas of the 'Elegy,' he made a definite and
memorable departure from the rigidity that was
threatening to deprive poetry of all its suppleness
and finer expression. In his diction he was unable
to escape with any certainty from the constraint

of his age. Poetry in his hands was still too often concerned with hearsay instead of vision, and, save at times when he gave himself up wholly to his better impulse, he was ready to lend his authority to the fustian rhetoric that did duty for style. We still have the 'attic warbler' and the 'fury Passions,' 'melting strains,' and the 'enchanting shell,' and we still find poetry masquerading in such dress as this:

> 'What idle progeny succeed
> To chase the rolling circle's speed,
>   Or urge the flying ball?'

There are, in short, many traces in Gray's poetry of a tradition against which he revolted but which he could not be expected to overcome at a stroke. But there are, scattered through his small volume of work, many instances of the poet's determination to express himself completely and with indifference to current standards. He could rival Pope himself on occasion in precision and the sublimation of mere reason, as for example in:

> 'all are men
> Condemned alike to groan,
> The tender for another's pain,
> The unfeeling for his own . . .'

or:

> 'where ignorance is bliss,
> 'Tis folly to be wise,'

or again in such a phrase as 'leave us leisure to be

good.' But he could also reach true dignity of style, a thing new to his time:

> 'Nor the pride, nor ample pinion
> That the Theban Eagle bear,
> Sailing with supreme dominion
> Thro' the azure deep of air,'

and:

> 'In gallant trim the gilded vessel goes;
> Youth on the prow and Pleasure at the helm,'

are notes for which he could find no example among his contemporaries save Collins. And he could, further, touch the pure simplicity of manner that he found discredited and rejected in the practice of the men that were then accepted as controllers of taste, and is yet the highest triumph of the poet's expression. He did this not only in such isolated passages as:

> 'The meanest floweret of the vale,
> The simplest note that swells the gale,
> The common sun, the air, the skies,
> To him are opening Paradise,'

but also, with very few lapses, throughout a whole poem. The 'Elegy Written in a Country Church-yard' has the distinction of being one of the few excellent poems in the language that are really popular. The qualities that have made it popular have, of course, nothing to do with Gray's position as a pioneer. They are those of tenderness and of clear distinction between sentiment and sentimentality, of intimacy with the beauty and change of earth, all set down without affectation and yet never meanly. It is a chapter of simple things which once again have gripped a poet by their loveliness and poignancy, and it is by virtue of this that it has won the affection of so many men; but it does, nevertheless, take on a new distinction when we realize that it was written at a time when these qualities were most grudgingly served by poetry. Gray had not a particularly rich imagination, but he was willing at times to allow what imaginative faculty he had free play. His power of vision was not of the highest, but in his more inspired moments he was careful to allow nothing to come between his vision and the thing seen. It has been charged against him that 'he never spoke out.' The criticism would not seem to be well considered. He did not, it is true, speak often, and he sometimes spoke without conviction. But it is not the least of his distinctions that at other times, when he was really moved to follow the guidance of his instinct, he was one of two men in his age who did speak out. He was not afraid to put on record the evidence of his imagination. If Gray saw blue hills, he called them blue and not bluish.

Wordsworth did Gray an injustice by placing him 'at the head of those who, by their reasonings, have attempted to widen the space of separation betwixt prose and metrical composition,' and adding that he was 'more than any other man curiously elaborate in the structure of his own poetic diction.' Even in his elaboration Gray was doing something to escape from a precision numbing in its formality, and, although Wordsworth rightly protested against much in the earlier poet's diction, he might have drawn his examples as aptly from almost any of Gray's contemporaries, who could not have defended themselves by an 'Elegy' or the passages of perfectly sincere and imaginative diction that are to be found in the Odes. Although Gray was not at all times a profitable servant, he was ever ready to acknowledge the lordship of the imagination, and it was ungenerous of Wordsworth to omit this fact from his reckoning. Johnson complained that he was 'tall by walking on tiptoe,' but the desire to be tall was in itself laudable, and not always unrewarded.

The poet's letters are not only delightful in their revelation of a most companionable personality, but they also contain many passages that show a clear-sightedness as to the general principles of his craft. It was natural enough that he should be mistaken as to Collins, and confused in his judgments of the work that was being done in his own day, even that he should at times be disloyal to his instincts in his own creation. The influence of Pope was too great for any man to resist without some hesitancy. But as soon as he began to consider the abstract nature of poetry he did so with admirable balance and insight. His professed essays on the art are concerned rather with the evolution of language and metrical form than with the cosmic spirit of poetry, but his correspondents might profit, if they were able, by many swift words of profound critical understanding. Speaking of description, he says, 'I have always thought that it made the most graceful ornament of poetry, but never ought to make the subject,' and his letters to Mason about that industrious writer's work abound in observations that are worthy of a better subject. It is clear from these flashes of criticism scattered through the letters that he had a finer understanding of his art than, perhaps, any man of his age, however inconsistently he may have applied his understanding in practice, and although this, again, does not add to his stature as poet, it gives some new distinction to his place in the history of letters.

The chief defect in his positive contribution to poetry is its unconcern with humanity. He peoples his poems with personages that are but rarely warm with life. Gray was not commonly fortunate in his choice of subjects. The Odes, which form the greater part of his work, each contain incidental and isolated passages that by their sudden rise to excellence of style or their clarity and intimacy of feeling are made memorable, but they do not command our interest either by their unity of conception, their sustained beauty of expression, or their nearness to our own experience. In the 'Elegy' alone among his more serious poems did he take a subject that by its simplicity and universality enabled him to write in complete accord with the impulse that was in him for direct and unstrained expression, and it is the 'Elegy' that we treasure as a complete poem, reading it from beginning to end when we turn back to it, not hastening forward for some rare glimpse of splendour that we know awaits us. In his lighter poems, notably 'The Long Story,' he attained something of this same warmth. His humour was always one of his most lovable qualities, and when he brings it to his poetry it is some compensation for the naturalness and depth that we miss in the Odes save at long intervals; nearly related as it is to the quick humanity that stirred him to utterance in the poem that popular affection has agreed with Dr. Johnson in proclaiming as his highest achievement.

SAMUEL TAYLOR COLERIDGE

WHEN the psychologist comes who shall attempt 'An Inquiry into the Visitations of Genius,' he might well adopt, as the sole basis of his investigation, 'Coleridge's Complete Poetical Works.'[1] We have them here in two volumes, admirably produced and edited, amounting to well over eleven hundred pages. By virtue of these, Coleridge, who was born in the year after Gray's death, and wrote his first known poem in 1787, takes a moderately distinguished place among the poets for whom we can only feel a certain compassionate reverence for their loyalty to an art that steadily refused to bestow any of its finer favours on their services. The eighteenth-century poets, those who were bound by, instead of transcending, their age, may not have been aware of their own rather painful limitations; but they were, at best, not allowed to know anything of the rarer ecstasy which is the poet's right, and to despise them is to despise a singularly unfortunate company of men. The good Mr. Akenside, had he lived a hundred years earlier, with all his desire and labour for poetry, might have set his heart dancing to some jolly song, in-

[1] *The Complete Poetical Works of Samuel Taylor Coleridge.* Edited by Ernest Hartley Coleridge. (Clarendon Press.)

stead of laboriously spending it on a forlorn hope; and even he made some honourable endeavour to bridge the darkest years that poetry has known since its beginning in England, with little enough of the poet's one true reward, whatever he may have had of praise. And Coleridge normally — save for some divine whim, always — is of this company. He remarks of one of his earliest compositions that it is not beyond the power of any clever schoolboy; that it is no more than a *putting of thought into verse*. That was the staple industry of Coleridge and his fellows. Through eleven hundred pages we find thought being put into verse; thought sometimes witty, sometimes dull, very often pompous and sentimental; but, save at one or two blessed intervals, never thought transfused into imagination and poetry. It shines in the gay little 'Ode in the Manner of Anacreon'; it is elephantine in things like the 'Religious Musings'; it struggles towards something rarer in stray lines like:

> 'And scatter livelier roses round,'

or stanzas such as:

> 'And oh! may Spring's fair flowerets fade,
> May Summer cease her limbs to lave
> In cooling stream, may Autumn grave
> Yellow o'er the corn-cloath'd glade;
> Ere ...'

or it trots merrily as in the lines 'Written After a

Walk before Supper.' It can become amazing, as in the 'Lines to a Friend, who Died of a Frenzy Induced by Calumnious Reports,' beginning:

> 'Edmund! thy grave with aching eye I scan ...'

it can perform admirable tricks, as in the epigram on Donne:

> 'With Donne, whose muse on dromedary trots,
> Wreathe iron pokers into true-love knots;
> Rhyme's sturdy cripple, fancy's maze and clue,
> Wit's forge and fire-blast, meaning's press and screw.'

And then, when the technique has been brought under easy control by long use, and the philosopher has matured, it can reach true sublimity in 'The Hymn before Sunrise' and 'Dejection.' Coleridge made all the poetic adventures approved by his time, and told of them generally as well as another, occasionally better. He wrote plays, too, and they make up one of the present volumes. In these he was Elizabethan by intention, and remained sealed of the eighteenth century in result. The sturdy strength that gave even Webster the mastery over his most unconsidered horrors was beyond the reach of the author of 'Remorse,' whose terror is the make-believe of a child. For the eighteenth-century Coleridge and his peers, the tragic clashing of the natural world and of humanity was not a great emotional ecstasy, but something of which to make a ceremony. They called it horrific, and were quite unmoved. Having none of the wisdom of imagination, they conceived the great wastes of tragedy to be a kind of fairyland, peopled by Shapes and Presences, who moved to a perpetual accompaniment of tremendous thunder. The external confusion of action that was utterly unimportant in the Elizabethans, because it had behind it a supreme spiritual unity, became in the hands of these men a meaningless end, instead of a riotous symbol.

And in all this our psychologist of the arts might find much to entertain him before beginning to write his treatise, which treatise would be provoked by certain poems that cover, perhaps, sixty pages of these two volumes. The years 1797–98 are curiously memorable ones in the history of poetry. A poet, moving smoothly enough along the appointed ways of his age, 'putting thought into verse' with some creditable success, in those years wrote ''The Ancient Mariner' and 'Christabel,' 'Frost at Midnight,' with its incomparable

> 'Therefore all seasons shall be sweet to thee,
> Whether the summer clothe the general earth
> With greenness, or the redbreast sit and sing
> Betwixt the tufts of snow on the bare branch
> Of mossy apple-tree, while the nigh thatch
> Smokes in the sun-thaw; whether the eave-drops fall
> Heard only in the trances of the blast,
> Or if the secret ministry of frost
> Shall hang them up in silent icicles
> Quietly shining to the quiet moon,'

and 'Kubla Khan.' Whatever achievement may be claimed by other poets, none can point to anything more manifestly drawn from a vigorous and enchanted imagination than these poems. Divine caprice has overthrown reason, and, line by line, we meet with adventures that none can foretell, and none can re-conceive. In accounting for the visitation, our æsthetician-psychologist need be distracted by no external circumstance. It has been suggested that Wordsworth's friendship inspired Coleridge to this strange new enthusiasm. It may, indeed, have helped to loose the poet's tongue; but it cannot, in any way, account for the miracle of the word that he was to utter. The best work of Coleridge's later years was a development of his earliest and normal manner and vision, with stray flashes of the wonder that only for one short period attained to clear and sustained expression. In 1817 it broke into one fitful gust in the eleven lines of 'The Knight's Tomb,' and at another date we get:

> 'So will I build my altar in the fields,
>   And the blue sky my fretted dome shall be,
> And the sweet fragrance that the wild flower yields
>   Shall be the incense I will yield to Thee,
> Thee only, God; and Thou shalt not despise
> Even me, the priest of this poor sacrifice.'

Even at his great period, Coleridge wrote with no certainty of genius. The three or four masterpieces were written at the same time as ineffective songs and pedestrian exercises, as untouched as possible by the heady inspiration of which he had tasted. What is yet stranger, the two moods and faculties may be found at this time in one poem, even in consecutive stanzas. That any poetic perception should be capable of setting these lines in the same poem is sufficiently amazing:

> "'Tis sweet to hear a brook, 'tis sweet
>   To hear the Sabbath-bell,
> 'Tis sweet to hear them both at once,
>   Deep in a woody dell.
>
> .   .   .   .
>
> 'So they sat chatting, while bad thoughts
>   Were troubling Edward's rest;
> But soon they heard his hard, quick pants,
>   And the thumping in his breast.'

But there is, at least, a saving interval between them, whilst the beauty of the second stanza of the following succeeds the ill-shapen doggerel of the first with perfect unconcern:

> 'And he had passed a restless night,
>   And was not well in health;
> The women sat down by his side,
>   And talked as 'twere by stealth.
>
> 'The Sun peeps through the close thick leaves,
>   See, dearest Ellen, see!
> 'Tis in the leaves, a little sun,
>   No bigger than your ee.'

Coleridge's visitation yielded him a small harvest of exquisite and essential poetry. He came face to face with song for one glorious season, and then, from time to time, he was vouchsafed a momentary glimpse that enabled his pen to touch the paper with something of the divine expectancy, but no more. Eleven hundred of these pages are as a prodigious monument, built in an outworn fashion, durable but dead. They are interesting to the analyst; they even have some intellectual excitement of their own at intervals; but it is all in verse that never sings or flies because of its own imaginative discovery. And the remaining pages — less than a hundred of them — are among the most marvellous treasures of poetry. It is a sheer delight to write down again such things as:

> 'The harbour-bay was clear as glass,
>   So smoothly it was strewn!
> And on the bay the moonlight lay,
>   And the shadow of the moon.'

And:

> 'The thin gray cloud is spread on high,
>   It covers but not hides the sky.
> The moon is behind, and at the full;
>   And yet she looks both small and dull.
> The night is chill, the cloud is gray:
> 'Tis a month before the month of May,
>   And the Spring comes slowly up this way.'

After all, the psychologist would but waste his pains. It is not to be explained. We can only watch Coleridge during those two years with 'admiration,' in Shakespeare's words:

> 'For he on honey-dew hath fed,
>   And drunk the milk of Paradise.'

WILLIAM WORDSWORTH

WILLIAM WORDSWORTH, the son of an attorney at Cockermouth in Cumberland, was born in 1770. He was educated at the Hawkshead Grammar School, and at Saint John's College, Cambridge, and after ten years of wandering, partly on the Continent, he went to live at Grasmere in the Lake Country, when he was just under thirty. His first home there was Dove Cottage, which has happily been preserved in its original simplicity and beauty under trust as a public property. Here he lived with his sister Dorothy, who remained in the household when he married Mary Hutchinson in 1802. About 1813, when he was appointed to the office of Distributor of Stamps for the County of Westmoreland, he moved to Rydal Mount, also in Grasmere, where he lived until his death in 1850. He was made Poet-Laureate on Southey's death in 1843.

As often happens in the case of poets who live long lives, the figure of Wordsworth that comes most readily to the mind is that of his old age. FitzGerald's 'Daddy Wordsworth' is recalled by the portraits that are generally known, and by the thought of the old poet, mild of aspect, and with eyes a little dulled after a lifetime of brooding among his Lakeland fastnesses, mumbling rhymes to himself as he shambles along the Grasmere roads. But this, revered figure though he rightly is, is not the Wordsworth that wrote himself among the greatest names of English poetry. It is well to remember the years from 1790 to something after 1800, when bright with passion and flaming with revolutionary ardour he tramped the Continent, meditated with intense devotion upon the principles of his art, formed with Coleridge the most important friendship of his life, published 'Lyrical Ballads' in collaboration with him and largely under his inspiration, and while in France, as recent research has shown, fell in love with a French girl by whom he had a daughter, who later inspired the lovely sonnet, 'It is a beauteous evening, calm and free.' The history, or rather the psychology, of this French episode is still rather obscure, but that does not much matter. The story itself is part of a youth surging with an eager vitality that we are apt to forget when we think of the Wordsworth of later days. The poet's youth has been described by himself in 'The Prelude.'

Wordsworth's interest to students of English poetry is twofold. Primarily he was a great poet, at his best to be ranked even with Shakespeare and Milton, and with hardly another to share that company. He was also a philosopher who in his critical Prefaces marked an epoch in poetic theory

in this country. It was in Wordsworth and Coleridge that what is called the Romantic Revival in
English Poetry first became fully articulate, and in
this Wordsworth was the pioneer of a new age.
But there is an aspect of his poetry that has not
been so fully considered. If he were the parent
stock from which much that is best in nineteenth-
century poetry derived, he was also the child of
the eighteenth-century poetry against which the
charges in his critical writings were chiefly directed.
His criticism is full of vision and understanding of
the nature of poetry, but it has to be allowed that
it was for the most part provoked by the excesses
and debasements that in the middle of the eighteenth century made ridiculous a kind of poetry
that, although it has fallen much out of fashion
in our own time, is nevertheless in its finer examples a very honourable kind, and the work of
poets of indisputable genius.

A reconsideration of eighteenth-century poetry
in general is one of the tasks to which contemporary criticism is now beginning to address itself with
great advantage. It is a commonly accepted fact
that in poets like Gray and Collins, and in some
less celebrated writers, such as the Countess of
Winchelsea, whom Wordsworth mentions with approval, there are definitely herald-notes of the new
romantic passion, the rediscovery of nature, that
worked to such great ends in Wordsworth and his

fellows. But there is far more in the matter than this. Wordsworth's professed aim was to purge poetry of its fustian, to base poetic diction once again upon the common speech of the time, to get rid of the bombast and false inflation to which the high example of Pope had degenerated in many of the poetasters of 1750. But Wordsworth was really preaching an established cause, though in doing it he might say much of inspired and lasting worth. Poetry in the practice of its masters was never in danger for long of forgetting the principles that Wordsworth enunciated with so much fervour, and in castigating the little and perverted talents of a generation that he could remember by hearsay, he overlooked the immense debt which he owed by inheritance to the finer spirits of that time. The influence of one poet upon another is always extremely difficult to define, but it is clear that a poet may often in subtle but important ways derive from poets whose work he does not know at all intimately. We are not sure, for example, how closely Wordsworth was acquainted with the more admirable poetry of the generation he pilloried, but to know both their poetry and his is to realize that consciously or unconsciously he drew from them far more freely both in manner and spiritual temper than he was willing to allow. In speaking of the Romantic Revival, Theodore Watts Dunton called it 'the Renaissance of Wonder,' and he called it exactly the right thing, or, at least, one of the right things. And in this quality Wordsworth was truly a pioneer. The magic, the sense of dim yet significant mystery in such a lyric as 'The Solitary Reaper,' were things beyond the achievement of the eighteenth-century poets, and, in their precise assembling of imaginative moods, new in English poetry. It could not be claimed for Wordsworth that he is a greater lyrist than the best Elizabethans, but his lyrical interpretation of Nature had in it a rapture of wonder that had never before been approached, save by the great lyrists of the seventeenth century in their religious intensity. And this quality is not only to be found in his short lyrical pieces, it pervades many of his ampler poems. But there is another quality in poetry, one that perhaps has not been greatly esteemed in our own day, which has nevertheless added, and will continue to add, many glories to English verse. It is, to put it crudely, a quality that resides in the clear philosophic statement of the poet's opinions about life, and in this quality the poetry of the eighteenth century was greatly distinguished, and it was a quality which descended from that poetry to Wordsworth in all its impressive dignity. Poems like 'The Spleen,' by Matthew Green (1737), and 'The Art of Preserving Health,' by Dr. John Armstrong (1744), have at the moment, it is to be supposed, very few readers.

And yet Green and Armstrong had one preëminent gift which will always make them very well worth reading; they could write. In their work the old sublime divinations of Shakespeare and his age had faded in the far distance, and on the other hand the Renaissance of Wonder had not yet begun to stir. But those poets, and there are many others equally good and equally neglected, can and do set down their personal reflections upon life, their sense of human character, their enthusiasms and their pity, and their moral independence, in clear and distinguished, and even at times in stirring, lines. Above all, they are hardly ever what they are commonly supposed to be — that is, dull. They fetch no wonders out of unknown heavens (as Keats did), nor do they strike suddenly to the deeps of unguessed-at knowledge (as Shakespeare did, or Donne). But they are poets, and they are aristocrats of verse, and no view of English poetry as a whole can ever be sound that underrates them. Whole tracts of Wordsworth's most impressive writing, not the brief notes of genius by which he is known to the multitude, but many pages which to the readers who study him with devotion are among his greatest gifts, are informed through and through with that eighteenth-century quality at its best, and it is, in fact, precisely the same kind of mind that would be horrified at the thought of reading 'The Spleen' or 'The Art of Preserving Health'

that finds much of the profoundest and most inde-
structible writing in Wordsworth himself dull.

Wordsworth's fame in the past forty years has
grown apace. In his own lifetime he was rightly
measured by a few, and generally honoured, but
he was far from attracting public attention in the
way that Byron and Scott, and, later, Tennyson,
did. Thirty years after his death, Matthew Arnold
in the 'Preface' to his famous Selection from
Wordsworth's poems, made for the Golden Treas-
ury Series, could say, no doubt with justice, that
even such popularity as Wordsworth had enjoyed
in his own time had steadily diminished. Arnold
pointed out, in 1879, that considered criticism of
Wordsworth had in later years nearly always been
sound, and had awarded the great poet his due,
but he also pointed out that the public had, in his
own words, 'remained cold, or, at least, undeter-
mined.' Arnold then proceeded very persuasively
to support his claim, which has been echoed in this
present essay, that Wordsworth's poetical performance was 'after that of Shakespeare and Milton, of which all the world now recognizes the
worth, undoubtedly the most considerable in our
language from the Elizabethan age to the present
time.' Arnold further argued that the principal
cause of public neglect was to be found in the mass
of inferior work in which the achievement of Wordsworth's genius had allowed itself to become ob-

scured, and in order that there should be no excuse
for neglect on these grounds thereafter, Arnold
made his own selection, and with flawless judgment.

Flawless judgment, that is to say, in the matter
of inclusion; there is nothing in Arnold's selection which does not obviously and immediately do
honour to Wordsworth. There is, however, the
question of exclusion, which is not quite so easily
answered. Arnold performed the greatest possible
service to Wordsworth's reputation, and his own
'Preface' has become a classic of English criticism.
This being so, any complaint must seem graceless.
At the same time, the scheme of Arnold's Selection
necessarily excluded a great deal of work which
the most ardent Wordsworthians would be loth to
surrender. For the general reading public who
ask, as they are quite entitled to do, for the quintes-
sence of a poet's work, Arnold's choice is impeccable. But in the case of a poet of the first rank
there will always be a certain number of readers
who are willing, and even anxious, to devote considerable time and care to an exhaustive study of
his whole nature and character. And for such a
reader who wishes so to understand Wordsworth,
Arnold's Selection, or any, must be incomplete. To
know 'The Solitary Reaper' and 'Michael' and
'The Leech-Gatherer' and the 'Ode on the Intima-
tions of Immortality' and 'I wandered lonely as a

cloud,' and the many pieces of that quality that
Arnold included, is to possess the fine flower of one
of the supreme English poetic gifts. But the reader
who recognizes in Wordsworth not only a great
lyric and elegiac poet, but one of the most significant spiritual and philosophic forces in the history
of English character, and thinks it worth while to
become familiar with that force in all its aspects,
must turn also to the long and often neglected
reaches of 'The Prelude' and 'The Excursion.'
There are many poets whose successes have been,
as it were, the happy accidents of minds not fundamentally preoccupied with poetry, and of these it is
well enough that the best should be chosen once
and for all, and the rest left alone. But Wordsworth, in his successes and failures alike, was a
poet first and last and through and through. His
whole nature was dedicated to all that poetry
means, and remembering the wide implications of
that claim, it may be said that it had no other concern whatever. So that when the last word is said,
Wordsworth is one of those poets who, while they
may rightly be presented to most people by their
chosen best, have, and always will have, the very
rare privilege of compelling from a few a careful
consideration of their work as a whole. And that
consideration, in Wordsworth's case, is apt, I think,
to discover that there is less really waste tissue in
his work than is commonly supposed. It is only the

very great poets who have a right to demand of us that we shall consider their achievement always in relation to their aim. From the work of lesser talents we are entitled to pick and choose, to judge each poem separately on its intrinsic merit by some external standard, but when we come to a poet of Wordsworth's stature it is at least worth while sometimes to ask ourselves, when we are inclined to question his practice, whether his judgment was not after all sounder than our own. Few, perhaps, of Wordsworth's most devoted admirers could claim to have read everything that he wrote. And yet, for some of us, to turn even to his most discredited pages is always to be prepared to find something that even this crowded world can very well afford to preserve.

PERCY BYSSHE SHELLEY

I

PERCY BYSSHE SHELLEY was drowned off the harbour of Leghorn on July 8, 1822, within a month of completing his thirtieth year. There has been more stupid and self-righteous chatter about his life, perhaps, than about that of any other great poet, with the exception of his friend Byron. He has vindicators in plenty, but he should need none. The conduct of his private affairs was not always blameless, if there should be anybody sufficiently free of fault himself to award the blame. That with all his shortcomings in these private affairs he was also generous, greatly beloved by his friends and at least one woman, of splendid character, and inspired always by an intense devotion to the abstract idea of liberty, there is ample evidence from a dozen sources. But in this, again, he was not really abnormal. At all times there are hundreds of young men about, sensitive, of swift impulses directed sometimes by good judgment, sometimes by bad, fine but not flawless in texture. Shelley, like any one of these, must have been an affectionate and attractive person to know, and no doubt sometimes a little disquieting if you happened to have your social standards too firmly fixed. And that, in summary, is all that need be said as to the man himself, except, perhaps, to add that his character in all directions bore a little the emphasis of genius. More freely, and at times, perhaps, a little more inexplainably than is common with a liberal and passionate youth, he defied and shocked the conventions of society, sometimes even the good ones. But he was one of the most Christian beings that ever walked earth. Yet whatever our conclusions may be about that life which burnt so fiercely and touched so many far points of delight and suffering, we must at least dissent from Professor Courthope's strangely inept exclamation that certain of Shelley's work will always 'draw the affection and sympathy of men towards their amiable and most unfortunate author.' The Shelleys of this world are not the misfortunes of omnipotent purpose.

When, however, Professor Courthope, in the same passage, refers to Shelley's vast and vague conceptions, he is on safer ground. Indeed, it is almost a truism of poetic criticism that Shelley's art yields less satisfactory results to analysis than, perhaps, that of any other of the English masters. Professor Saintsbury bluntly says that such analysis is futile, and that the worst thing Shelley ever wrote is better reading than the best thing ever written about him. In a way it may be said that no poet has made surer advance from the beginning to the end of his life in the technical control of his material than did Shelley, and yet he is almost alone in having been able to impress the peculiar quality of his genius and vision on his earliest and very immature efforts no less surely than on his later masterpieces. 'The Demon of the World,' for example, and 'Alastor,' not to mention the earlier 'Queen Mab,' and even less assured things, can hardly be called good poems by any reckoning. They are loose in construction, vague always in outline, uncertain in intellectual, if not in emotional, purpose, and scattered throughout with extraordinary patches of mere verbal insensitiveness. And yet, suffusing the whole there is the peculiar Shelleyan flush of beauty which signs almost any fragment of his work as surely as Milton's supremacy of style signs his own work in, say, 'Lycidas.' And the quality of that beauty was constant until the end. It became much more exactly subdued to the terms of poetic art in such things as the simple wonder of 'Adonais' and, in 'Epipsychidion,' that marvellous snaring of an almost inconceivably subtle emotion. But the life and ardour remain those of 'Queen Mab.' The frustration and protest and yearning, even the despair, which are so largely the staple of his poetic material, are translated always into shimmering rainbow hazes. And Shelley's prophetic argument is peculiar in that it is one which cannot be argued about. His art is much more one of colour than of form, of colour which in its nebulousness often defies our understanding, and of which sometimes the only thing that we are certain is its purity.

It is, of course, impossible to state the whole question in a word like this. It would be absurd to suggest that Shelley had no sense of form. His dramas and 'Adonais' alone would make it ridiculous to do so. But the austere architecture that is the chief poetic glory of Milton and Keats and Wordsworth seems to have been little his aim. Nor was the discipline in the detail of his art always as exact as is common with men of his greatness. His work is marked, as that of no other great poet, with frequent heavy-handed use of words. He writes almost like a divine improvisor who is lucky most of the time, but who cannot stay to question his luck when it fails him. And in the bad moments he will use phrases that have not the poetic nerve in them at all. A line like 'I think I never was impressed so much' is merely flat and may perhaps be excused in a long poem. But when a page later we read

> 'His child had now become
> A woman; such as it has been my doom
> To meet with few...'

we pass from mere flatness to an insensitiveness which is hardly credible in a genius so rare. And Shelley's poems contain a great number of examples of this kind of thing. In a word, he, of the great English poets, is the most given to lapses into downright bad writing. And, on the other hand, as might be expected, his most memorable moments are those in which a concept of the mind is phrased not in what may be called inspired statement, such as we find on every page of Shakespeare, but in some perfect image which gives us the delight of realizing vision apart from any philosophic consideration. When he wants to put a desolated country before us, he does it by saying merely

'Blue thistles bloomed in cities...

The imagination working in that particular kind could achieve nothing more consummate than that. It is far less often that he stirs us with the other kind, the Shakespearean kind, of utterance. It is seldom that we are moved by such things in his verse as

'Most wretched men
Are cradled into poetry by wrong,
They learn in suffering what they teach in song.'

And this is the more strange when one considers how explicitly philosophic in intention Shelley's poetry was. Keats, in a well-known passage, says to Shelley:

I received a copy of *The Cenci*, as from yourself, from Hunt. There is only one part of it I am judge of — the poetry and dramatic effect, which by many spirits nowadays is considered the Mammon. A modern work, it is said, must have a purpose, which may be the God. An artist must serve Mammon; he must have 'self-concentration' — selfishness, perhaps. You, I am sure, will forgive me for sincerely remarking that you might curb your magnanimity, and be more of an artist, and load every rift of your subject with ore.

That was well enough and one sees exactly the mood in Keats from which it came, although it may be pertinently remarked that Keats was in his last work clearly moving towards just some such 'purpose' himself. However that may be, there the purpose was in Shelley from the beginning, dominating his whole poetic career for good or bad, and it must be believed, in spite of much modern critical opinion to the contrary, that it was for good. Shelley very desperately did want to make the world a better place. He wanted to sing it into being a better place. He wanted to instruct people, he upbraided the tyrants, he denounced the betrayal of love fiercely and on every occasion. He preached and he moralized, and he did these things with determination, looking upon himself as a poet with a mission, one that he would have pursued had he lived to be seventy. Being a great poet, he was justified in his purpose, and he showed, just as all the other great poets have done, only rather more expressly than they, that some such purpose in the poet's mind is really the only soil out of which complete artistic creation can spring. This does not mean that a poet must be always making us conscious of his purpose, and it may be admitted that Shelley at times was a little too insistent, but the purpose must be there or there will be no poetry. Sometimes nowadays we see poets scolded by writers of criticism for taking their poetry very seriously. It is a strange perversity that can find offence here, provided always that purpose is subdued to art as it was in Shelley. It would be interesting to read the reception that would be given by such writers to a poet who should to-day preface his work thus:

The Poem which I now present to the world is an attempt from which I scarcely dare to expect success, and in which a writer of established fame might fail without disgrace. It is an experiment on the temper of the public mind, as to how far a thirst for a happier condition of moral and political society survives, among the enlightened and refined, the tempests which have shaken the age in which we live

— and much more in the same strain. In fact, this particular school of criticism ought on every count to throw Shelley over altogether. It is fortunate for the art of poetry that Shelley would very happily survive the event, and we should be enlightened by an honest piece of self-revelation.

II

If, as is not unlikely, some people may ask why more books on Shelley, they cannot be better an-

swered than by Shelley's own words quoted by
Mrs. Campbell at the end of her book:

A great poem is a fountain for ever overflowing with
the waters of wisdom and delight; and after one person
and one age has exhausted all its divine effluence which
their peculiar relations enable them to share, another
and yet another succeeds, and new relations are ever
developed, the source of an unforeseen and an uncon-
ceived delight.

And it may be said at once that both these books [1]
are valuable additions to the formidable body of
Shelley literature, and that they may be read with
profit even by the poet's best-informed students.
It is, indeed, as will be shown, those who know
Shelley's life and works most intimately who will
be likely to get most advantage from the books
now before us.

When two volumes on one subject appear at the
same time the critic is naturally tempted to compare them with each other. The temptation is
generally one to be resisted, since more often than
not there will be no useful points of comparison.
But in the present instance Mrs. Campbell and
M. Maurois (admirably translated by Miss Ella
D'Arcy) do, in their defects as well as in their qualities, decidedly measure and supplement each

[1] *Shelley and the Unromantics.* By Olwen Ward Campbell. London:
Methuen & Co.

Ariel. A Shelley Romance. By André Maurois. Translated by
Ella D'Arcy. London: John Lane.

other. Mrs. Campbell's book is probably the best organizing of the Shelley material that has ever been made. And yet it has many faults, and the chief of them is that the term 'organizing' is not an exact one to apply to it. Mrs. Campbell has acquired a familiarity with Shelley's poetry and every record that has been left of his life, that has now clearly become an intimate habit of her mind. Her interpretation of the poems and data is, moreover, in almost every respect convincing. It is impossible to read her work without having great respect for her own intelligence and gift of sympathy. She says hardly a thing about Shelley that is not at once perfectly documented and finely conceived. But her book somehow leaves a cumulative impression that is not as incisive as it ought to be. Putting it down, we nearly always found on returning to it that we had lost our place. It is not that the actual writing is bad; on the contrary, most of it is extremely good. Nor, on the other hand, is it merely that practically all the material that Mrs. Campbell is investigating is after all pretty well known already, and that on returning to her pages we are not quite sure for the moment whether it is here or elsewhere that we have already read what is in front of us. The difficulty is that Mrs. Campbell, with all her unusual gifts as a writer, which we gladly recognize, and which are turned in this book to really valuable account, seems to lack the one faculty of giving her work the crowning elucidation of an easily mastered design. It is a pity, because the defect may deprive of some of its proper influence what is in substance worthy to be put in the front rank of critical literature.

In three other respects Mrs. Campbell's book is provocative. The chapters devoted to literary criticism seem inadequate, chiefly, perhaps, because they are summary and out of proportion to the biographical matter of the volume, which is exhaustive. This is not to say that Mrs. Campbell does not make many extremely acute observations upon Shelley's poems and upon poetry in general, although she occasionally allows herself what she must surely realize in her heart is so cheaply epigrammatic a turn as: 'No really great poet is a poet purely of Nature. The eighteenth century was alive with poets of Nature; the twentieth century is dead with them.' We have little room in which to justify by examples our opinion, good or bad, of Mrs. Campbell's critical powers, but as an instance of many valuable things that she says may be given this, of Wordsworth:

He made the mistake of supposing that the suffering and emotions of an old dalesman are *ipso facto* more stirring and instructive than those of a man in a high position — a king or any heroic public figure, — and this is really an anti-social, and thus an inartistic, conception.

Secondly, in the more important part of her

book, the author occasionally disregards her own
excellent principle of tolerant understanding, as in
her treatment of Mary Shelley, from whose own
words she quotes the pathetic request, 'Do not
awaken the deep waters that are full of briny
bitterness. I never wish anyone to dive into the
secret depths,' and at the same time scrutinizes her
character with what seems to be something less
than perfect charity. This observation leads us to
our third and more general reservation about the
book, and, indeed, about almost all such books,
which is that in matters of character they are apt to
assume that the available evidence, however ample
it may be, is more conclusive than it really is. We
seem to know an immense amount about Shelley
and the bewildering group of people of whom
he was the most divinely appointed spirit. Mrs.
Campbell certainly knows more about them than
any of us, and she would no doubt at once challenge
the word 'bewildering.' In the light of her devoted
learning and natural gifts of perception they do not
seem bewildering to her, she is clear that she knows
them precisely. But does she? Might not a week at
Edinburgh, and another week at Marlowe, and a
share in the sad little journey with the donkey, and
a month or two at Pisa and San Torenzo modify
her impressions, and even revise some of them? We
cannot tell these things; but we are convinced that
minute investigations of character, when they are

concerned not with creative purposes but with the history of people who actually lived, should always be made with a fuller sense of their own necessarily tentative nature than they generally are. At the same time it is to be gratefully admitted that Mrs. Campbell has almost certainly in the main fixed the truth about the kind of being that Shelley was, and it is in this fundamental respect that her book has a commanding advantage over M. Maurois's witty and perspicuous narrative.

'Ariel' succeeds just where Mrs. Campbell's book relatively fails. It, too, takes the known facts of Shelley's life, and with very little invention or trimming presents them in plain narrative form. But M. Maurois's handling of his material is masterly. The outline of his romance is perfectly contrived. We leave 'Ariel' with an exact realization of all that its author intended to say. And this is said wittily, and in its incidental aspects with great psychological shrewdness and humour. But in one essential respect it leaves us unsatisfied. The Shelley that M. Maurois presents is chivalrous, a great poet, a charming gentleman. But behind this presentation there is all the time the suspicion that he is being patronized. In M. Maurois's hero there is always uncomfortably a touch of the inspired idiot. He is considered with great tenderness, and even, in spite of the irony which we are told on the cover of the book Mr. Arnold Bennett found side-splitting, with affection. But it is the affection, we cannot sometimes help feeling, of a benevolent guardian for a delightful and inspired child who is not quite right in his head. We would not be unjust to M. Maurois. His book is, as we say, in its kind, something very like a masterpiece, and he would very likely hotly disclaim any such intention as we have attributed to him. But the feeling persists, nevertheless, as we read the book, and we no longer have any patience with the inspired idiot conception of Shelley in however flattering terms it may be presented.

It is a book one is glad to have read for its many adroitly intuitive strokes, and it, too, is a worthy contribution to the subject. But it is not, for example, a book we should care to give to a youngster with a developing love of literature as his first insight into the character of one of the loveliest figures in English poetry. And for this reason we say that it is rather for the informed than the uninformed; just as Mrs. Campbell's book is so for the reason that its readers, unless they can organize her material as they go along from their own knowledge, will be apt to find their impressions rather nebulous, which is always discouraging to the student. But for the initiated M. Maurois will provide much intellectual delight in a by no means emotionally arid atmosphere, and Mrs. Campbell a noble and imaginative piece of interpretation.

MODERN INSTANCES

... the morning brings
As true a song as any yesterday.

WILLIAM CORY [1]

I

WILLIAM CORY — he was William Johnson by birth and took the name of Cory in 1872 for family reasons — was born in January, 1823, and died in 1892, a few months before reaching the age of seventy. The centenary of his birthday, therefore, falls in the present year, and it is fitting that the occasion should not pass unhonoured in a Society devoted to the interests of Literature, and particularly by the Chair in that Society chiefly concerned with poetry. For Cory was a poet, of slight and desultory genius, writing and publishing very little verse, and yet with a secure though slender claim to 'a permanent place,' as the 'Dictionary of National Biography' puts it, 'among English lyrists.' He is in that work wrongly credited with several volumes of poems. In fact he published, apart from a few classical experiments composed chiefly in the nature of school exercises, but two small pamphlets of verse. The first of these, 'Ionica,' [2] appeared in 1858, from the house of Smith Elder, and it was followed in 1877 by the privately

---

[1] Read to the Royal Society of Literature from the Chair of Poetry.
[2] *Ionica* had been preceded in 1843 by the prize poem *Plato*, which obtained the Chancellor's medal at Cambridge in that year.

printed 'Ionica II,' containing a further twenty-five poems. Both of these little volumes appeared anonymously. In 1891 he added a few new poems to the old ones, and published them together, retaining the original title, with George Allen, the authorship still being unacknowledged.

Small as the volume of Cory's poems is, it is yet considerably smaller when it is reduced to those pieces by which his reputation as a lyrist is established. For the most part the verses are marked more clearly by personality than by lyric success. Cory himself was always shy about their publication, considering them to be rather the occasional notes of personal intimacies and circumstance, not designed for a wider public. Having been a boy at Eton himself, he left Cambridge after a brilliant career to take up a mastership in that school, and he remained there for twenty-seven years. Of the devotion and the beauty of character which he brought to his task, and kept unspoilt through the long term of its exercise, more is to be said, but it may here be noted that many of his verses are the charming but slight and closely personal record of the contacts and occasions of those years. His poetic gift, however, could be used to much more general effect, and lying among the more occasional pages of his book are to be found others that will continue to delight the readers that they may find. 'Mimnermus in Church,' 'Amaturus,' 'A

Queen's Visit,' 'After reading "Maud,"' 'A Cruise,'
'A Fable,' 'A Ballad for a Boy,' 'Barine,' 'Mir ist
Leide,' 'Remember,' 'An Apology,' 'Reparabo,'
'Prospero,' and 'Heraclitus,' seem to me to be the
pick of these, and they make a little sheaf fine
enough in quality to keep Cory's name fresh in
English poetry. Here are two of them:

REPARABO

The world will rob me of my friends,
　　For time with her conspires;
But they shall both to make amends
　　Relight my slumbering fires.

For while my comrades pass away
　　To bow and smirk and gloze,
Come others, for as short a stay;
　　And dear are these as those.

And who was this? they ask; and then
　　The loved and lost I praise:
'Like you they frolicked; they are men;
　　Bless ye my later days.'

Why fret? the hawks I trained are flown:
　　'Twas nature bade them range;
I could not keep their wings half-grown,
　　I could not bar the change.

With lattice opened wide I stand
　　To watch their eager flight;
With broken jesses in my hand
　　I muse on their delight.

And, oh! if one with sullied plume
　　Should droop in mid career,

My love makes signals: 'there is room,
Oh bleeding wanderer, here.'

HERACLITUS

They told me, Heraclitus, they told me you were dead,
They brought me bitter news to hear and bitter tears to shed.
I wept as I remember'd how often you and I
Had tired the sun with talking and sent him down the sky.

And now that thou art lying, my dear old Carian guest,
A handful of grey ashes, long, long ago at rest,
Still are thy pleasant voices, thy nightingales, awake;
For Death, he taketh all away, but them he cannot take.

'Heraclitus' is both Cory's best and his most
celebrated poem. In its company some of the other
pieces will survive, as they should do, but without
it they would probably fall into neglect. In reading the lovely lines

'I wept as I remember'd how often you and I
Had tired the sun with talking and sent him down the sky . . .'

it is interesting to recall a passage in Lord Lyttelton's Elegy on his wife published in 1747:

'In vain I look around
O'er all the well-known Ground
My Lucy's wonted Footsteps to descry;
Where oft we us'd to walk,
Where oft in tender Talk
We saw the Summer Sun go down the Sky.'

'Heraclitus,' translation or rendering though it
is, becomes a perfect English lyric, and while some
of Cory's other poems are worthy of a place beside
it, none can be said quite to match it.

II

WHILE, however, the claims of Cory's verse may, in their own modest though distinguished way, be readily allowed, he gave little of his time or energy to poetical composition, and it was not as a poet that he most readily expressed himself. He belonged to a type that we are tempted to consider as being peculiarly English. A liberal classical education and a fine general culture combined in him to produce a mind observant, inquisitive, and lucidly critical. This is admirable enough but not uncommon. The uncommon thing is when such a mind, constantly exercised as it is apt to be in a wide range of insistent but ephemeral interests, retains a genuinely unsophisticated delight in profound emotional simplicities; when, in other words, the poetry of a mind is not destroyed by the constant application of affairs, by keeping abreast of current events. And this happy constitution of mind, though it must always be rare, is, it might seem, commoner in Englishmen than in most. What is meant is something far more than the mere educated interest in art and letters which may be found often enough in men of affairs the world over. It is the gift of submitting all events and institutions, as they have to be dealt with, not only to history, but to the imaginative wisdom which is the flower of the universal mind — in fact to poetry. It is, further, a gift that moves beyond a sense of this admirable necessity into the regions of independent creation. Our literature is rich in the names of men who have achieved great distinction as writers, without having been devoted wholly to the calling of letters. Spenser, Sidney, Bacon, Marvell — the succession could be shown down to men like Lord Morley and Lord Rosebery and Sir Ronald Ross in our own time. It is true that the achievement of such writers is generally rather in the fields of critical or philosophical than of imaginative literature, though there are obvious exceptions. The reason is plain. Men of affairs, whether in commerce or the professions or politics, when the demands of their calling are satisfied, can very rarely be expected to have a surplus energy equal to imaginative creation. The surprising thing is that so many of them have, if not this energy, at least a reserve of power left that enables them to contribute seriously, by the best standards, to literature of a high, if not often of the highest order.

William Cory, in the natural movements of his mind, was a great man of affairs. This claim may seem to be extravagant, and remembering the seclusion of his Eton mastership, to be followed by a yet greater seclusion, when at the age of forty-seven he became a country squire, never again to take up any more active occupation, it is clear that

I do not mean a great man of affairs in the ordinary sense. I said in the natural movements of his mind. By circumstance Cory was a diligent schoolmaster, a lonely and fastidious scholar, a gentle and very occasional poet. But by instinct he belonged to, and by his interests he lived in, the great world of affairs, the world of statesmanship and political crises, of wars and social reforms, of national designs and industry, with an intense and persistent ardour. Though he was not a man of action, either under arms or in office, he spent as much energy as though he had been closely engaged himself. Almost his only literary production, apart from his poems, and a long series of letters, written for the most part to men who had been under him at Eton, was a journal which he kept, and of which he says himself, 'I do every vacation write a genuine original book, my journal for about three readers. . . . I believe every man of sensibility might with some advantage do this, omitting all megrims, grumblings and sneers.' This journal, with a considerable selection of the letters, was privately published in 1897 for something over twenty subscribers. How many copies of the book were printed I do not know, but it has become a rare volume. A popular edition is, I believe, now in contemplation. Both journal and letters, which together run to nearly six hundred pages and make very attractive reading throughout, are packed with observation and criticism of the dominant personalities and events of the Victorian stage. Literature is a constant subject of his reflection, but he confines himself usually in this matter to summary judgments, while his commentary upon current politics in all their ramifications is minutely argued and widely informed. And in this fact lies the explanation, perhaps, of Cory's meagre productivity as a poet. He was in his journal and letters (he probably was also in his personal relations) an immense talker, and while he was a match for anyone in scholarship, and historical perspective, and literary knowledge, when these were needed, he yet more freely talked of the great network of current politics and affairs with exhaustive information on his subject. And such talk inevitably dissipates the concentration necessary to sustained poetic production. In his later years he speaks of the renewed delight, when an occasional visitor of intellectual parts went to see him in his Devonshire seclusion, of improvising original opinions in conversation. The delight is one in which we all at times fondly imagine we share, but the creative mind indulges it with any freedom only at great risk, while to the true talker it becomes an almost daily necessity. And Cory was a true talker. The improvization of which he speaks was never irresponsible or unrelated to conviction or standards, but it was improvization in the special sense that creation is not.

His aims were not brilliance or dialectic victory; indeed, he tells us at the age of twenty-four that the true purpose of discussion is to make 'a minute comparison of minds without argument' and again twenty years later, that the use of Cambridge debates was 'to lay minds fairly alongside of each other.' But none the less this preoccupation of his with affairs did lead him constantly, as it always does, into attaching undue importance to the things of sound and fury that in the long run signify but little more than nothing. His journal pages are full of earnest and even heated arguments that have long since been swept away in the litter of forgotten controversy, and are now only redeemed from mere dulness by the faintly surviving charm of Cory's presentation. These parts of the journal show us a man touched by that garrulousness of intellect which, even though it be truly of intellect, forbids the deeper and simpler contemplations of poetry, and we have to return to other parts of the journal and to 'Ionica' to be reminded that Cory was a poet at all.

III

AND of Cory's essential poetic character there is in these other parts of the journal abundant evidence to place beside 'Ionica.' In his vacations and in the freedom of his later years he travelled a good deal, and the accounts in his journal of the places that he visits are vivid with observation and allusion. Association was inevitably precious to a mind so richly stored. 'What travelling,' he asked, 'is like that which takes one to the haunts of poets and the sanctuaries of historical nations.' The common heritage of poets, a sense of beauty's transience, is strong in him. In Westminster Abbey, he tells us that he is far more moved by the epitaphs than by the sermons, 'implicitly believing that the irrecoverable souls were as fair as the marbles say they were, longing to know them, pitying them for being dead, pitying their kinsfolk who lost them so long ago.' When he is abroad, however, it is not so much in the brilliant descriptive strokes that enliven his journal that we find the essentially poetic character asserting itself, as in a passion that unifies the experiences of his travel. In Cory's case the passion was patriotism, 'the sweep and splendour of England's war,' as Sir Henry Newbolt puts it in his fine elegy, the war being one that transcends the local habitation of the battlefield. In almost everything he saw abroad, of peoples and customs and institutions, he found some reflection of England's honour or failure, and his jealousy that she should nobly fulfil what he conceived to be her mission in the world was constant. Whether or not his political ambitions for his country made for general human good to the degree that he believed we need not discuss here, but that they burned in his spirit with an absolute purity there can be no doubt. The only misgiving — almost certainly an unjust and ungenerous one — we ever have in the presence of his passionate loyalty is when he, from his gentle seclusion, urges others to fierce and dangerous action. Given the circumstances, Cory would, we are sure, without hesitation have died for his country himself, but the misgiving persists because the answer is not quite complete. However this may be, in hardly any other way do we ever question the character that presents itself in the journal and letters.

Lord Esher, in his newly published volume, 'Ionicus,' is right in attributing Mr. A. C. Benson's assertion that Cory's was 'probably one of the most vigorous and commanding minds of the century' to friendly exaggeration, but there can be no doubt that it would be difficult to exaggerate the influence that he had upon his pupils, both at Eton and in their later life. And these pupils included a large group of men who came to the highest distinction in the public life of their time. The 'Letters and Journals' are full of communication with or reference to Lord Rosebery, Lord Balfour, Alfred Lyttelton, and a score of other men whose names are less remembered now but who were of equal eminence in their day. With many of these he kept in constant touch till the end of his life, as Lord Esher's volume, containing as he says only a quarter of the letters Cory wrote to him, shows, and Lord Esher's devotion to his old master is clearly characteristic of many such life-long loyalties in other pupils. With many of his Eton boys Cory corresponded before the end of their school days, when they were away on vacation or sick-leave, and he had the great gift of talking to them already without the slightest intellectual condescension. Nothing could be more charming than the unaffected gravity with which he can ask a boy of fifteen for his advice and opinion.[1]

Although he was a brave and far from unhappy man, Cory after the first brilliant promise of his Cambridge days always carried with him something of a sense of failure. He was never robust, and he was so near-sighted as to be almost blind at any distance, until he delightedly discovered the use of a spy-glass. He was very well aware, too, of the constraint upon achievement that the routine of Eton meant. He did not complain, he was, indeed, on the whole satisfied that the ways of his

[1] In 1898 the Oxford Press published a pamphlet, *Hints for Eton Masters*, by W. J ——, taken from a manuscript journal of 1862. It is full of wise counsel to pedagogues, and a charming product of Cory's lively style. The following note upon not giving sufficient credit for work well done in school is characteristic. 'If we cheered those who play our bowling in school well, as heartily as we cheer our batsmen at Lord's, I think there would be a little more zeal amongst our young students.'

life were happily chosen, but we feel all the time
that he would have liked to have some wider ad-
ministrative power, that he would have liked to
impress his scholarship more brilliantly upon his
age, that he would have liked to accomplish more as
a writer, that, above all, he would have liked to set
his name among the heroes that he worshipped.
'The cavalry weapon against unbroken infantry
is the horse. Let one man make a hole, live or die
in it, the square is pierced. The Germans did it at
Salamanca. I would like to end my life that way,
if the square were made of Russian diplomats,
motherless, wifeless, and sisterless.' So he wrote
when he was over fifty, in the spirit in which as a
young master at Eton he had taken the boys out
of the classroom to see the Guards marching down
the street, with the admonition, 'Brats, the British
army!' But he was early aware of the narrowness
of his destiny, sometimes poignantly, sometimes
humorously. When he was twenty-five the modern
history professorship at Cambridge fell vacant, and
his name seems to have been mentioned. He notes,
'I should never be man enough for a place like
Cambridge, but at a second-rate university I
should make a good history professor as things go.'
At forty he recalls the eager ambitions of early
days, when he little thought that after all he 'was
to be nothing but a third-rate grammar-monger.'
And a year or two later there is this entry in the

journal: 'There are many days, weeks, months, in which I feel like a fungus in a retired part of a kitchen garden — forgotten, left out, useless. Then comes a torrent of notices more or less indicative of regard or consideration, and I am lifted into the honours of a conspicuous dandelion. . . . At luncheon appeared my pupil with a note from his mother asking me to dinner, so that the dandelion became a dahlia.'

By the time he was forty he seems to have put ambition by. He notes his departure from a country house thus, 'Lady M. gave me a fragrant geranium leaf at parting, and the boy saw me off; and in two hours I had relapsed into my average dulness.' About the same time he remarks, 'A family that knows illness has the due chiaroscuro,' but for himself he has found 'something that looks very like health . . . and I have sometimes been very nearly free from self-pity.' Self-pity, indeed, was not one of his indulgences. At the age of fifty, on returning from Eton, he took over Halsdon, the small family estate in Devonshire, of which he had acquired a lease. 'I am not well; and half my time I meditate the ceremony of dying, but the other half I bud with schemes for the enjoyment of my liberty.' But by then his character was mellowed, and his mind, disciplined to its own sphere, 'in beautiful order,' as he said of one of his own pupils. From his hermitage at Halsdon he can still fret and

argue about affairs when he is provoked by some
ministerial stupidity, or what he takes to be some
heresy in an old pupil, but his daily habit is now
one of gentle and often idyllic contemplation, and a
lyric delight in the seasons of his little farm and his
squirearchic duties. His wish to own twelve cows,
expressed many years before at Eton, has come
true, and the shrubs and walks are a serious business, with fifty little rhododendrons from Windsor
Park — 'the Queen's own' — to be planted, and
occasional distributions of plants and flowers
among gardens less favoured than his own.

And now it is that all the Virgilian sweetness in
him asserts itself. There are passages in the journal
that have an exquisite satisfaction of phrase, such
as when years before he spoke of the codling tarts
at his Eton feasts.

He writes in a letter of August, 1874;

Robert and I last night attacked the hornets who live
in the hollow tree on which hangs the gate through which
goes Grizzle to fetch grist from Dolton Mill.

Robert was in the poncho or chasuble and a muslin
veil. He directed me; I held a long stick with a brimstone rag. Hornets now and then dropt into burning
straw — they were as stupid as the French in Stras-
bourg, and made no sortie.

To-night we assist a more nimble sort of enemies,
'apple-drones,' or wasps, close to the stable. R. goes to
the town to buy brimstone. I have prepared a sea-kail
pot which is to go over the hole, and a dozen dead tree-

lets — 'our failures' (as Beau Brummell said of his cra-
vats). I hope we shall not burn the thatch of the
stable. . . .

There has been a burst of new flowers, not weeds, and
birds singing and owls talking to each other since you
went.

He talks of the children who are his friends, and
says that the 'choice thing for girls is to go up the
ladders and peep at the pigeons' nests to count the
eggs therein.' And then again,

I have four lambs, born in March, quite untameable.

I have a friend among the percher birds. He comes to
breakfast; but he won't let me come near enough to see
whether he is a robin or a chaffinch.

I miss the stable-boy, Jan, who used to show me the
nests. . . .

He has a party in the barn which costs four
pounds. 'Just compare that with a London or even
a Dolton rectory dinner-party, and then compare
the aggregate of impressions made at the two,
imagine the sweet little thrill it gives a Dolton girl,
of the humblest birth, to come down and sing to
us "Who is Sylvia?" . . . Whereas when your rich
people go to a dinner-party they think no more of
it than I do of brushing my hair.' He stayed at
Halsdon until 1878, when he was fifty-five, receiving old Eton and Cambridge friends as visitors
from time to time, faithfully discharging his local
responsibilities, and forming very genuine attach-

ments with his farm servants, some of whom he afterwards pensioned with no particular obligation and out of small means. His generosity was always punctilious. Directly he could afford it he gave up his Cambridge fellowship thinking it improper to be an unnecessary charge on the College funds. Years before, writing to a young correspondent from Eton, after a friendly lecture on University economy, he had concluded, 'If you want money to hire a coach, mathematical or otherwise, I beg that you will not take it from the other claims, but let me advance it, and you may repay all such sums, £100 if you like, when you are a prosperous man ten years hence or so.' He went from Halsdon to Madeira, where he surprised his friends by marrying. He had one son, Mr. Andrew Cory, who is still alive, to whom as a child the letters contain many touching references. 'When I sit, as I do every night on duty, by Andrew's bedside, I am truly content, yet I weep every day to think of having to leave him.' That was in 1881. William Cory lived another ten years, coming back to London and dying in Hampstead in 1892. His later years, in spite of precarious health, lost nothing in shrewdness of mind or buoyancy of spirit. His excursions in political criticism and prophesy were as penetrating as ever, and often borne out by the event. 'Rule Britannia' was a favourite tag in his letters. He published the two volumes of 'A Guide to Modern English History,' about the time he left Halsdon, and the new edition of 'Ionica' the year before he died. These, apart from a few occasional papers, make the sum of his literary production. He read eagerly and widely, fiction, drama, history, biography, and Lord Esher tells us of a constant flow of books from house to house: 'If you are in cash I advise you to buy it before it gets out of print, the Oxford Press, five volumes, Hill's Boswell, a monumental book. When I have got through Lecky, I am going to read Pollock on Torts.'

IV

LITERATURE, it goes without saying, was a constant and presiding interest in Cory's life. He might say, 'Our literature is a supreme blessing to us, yet I find in my loneliness still more comfort in the sustained action of our nation: Graham at Malaga shying stones at the assassins, and Baker trampling on the demons of the Equator, and Glover raising recruits on the Gold Coast. . . . all this is real meat and drink to me,' but his enthusiasm for letters was more fundamental than this might suggest. The literary judgments that he gives us are, as I have said, seldom as closely argued as his political criticism. They are as often as not merely a statement of likes and dislikes, but knowing Cory we may find a mere catalogue of his preferences instructive. His taste was fine, but often, as it seems to us, strangely capricious — that is to say he was never in danger of liking a bad thing, but he was often iconoclastic and even merely prejudiced. His prejudices were sometimes coloured by political considerations, which made him see in Shelley 'a Bashi Bazouk and an enemy of England,' or by a certain genteel morality which led him into the ineffable stupidity of dismissing Burns as a sot, though he pays tribute to the Scot's genius elsewhere, and an immense and sometimes almost overweening faith in his own age, which made him assert with great conviction that Tennyson was to be rated far above Milton. Tennyson was indeed his hero in poetry. 'It is now exactly forty years since Tennyson has been to me the light and charm of my poor life'. And again, 'Tennyson is the sum and product of the art that began with Homer. I cannot say that he is greater than Homer; but he fills my soul and makes the best part of forty years of manhood that I have gone through.' Wordsworth meant much to him, though apparently a good deal less than Tennyson:

Mat Arnold's paper in 'Macmillan' on 'Wordsworth' hits the nail on the head now and then: he names as his favourites 'Michael,' 'Highland Reaper,' and the 'Fountain'; he did not seem to see that most of the gems of Wordsworth are rather slight things to build so great a name upon: a man who tries to make a big thing, and fails again and again, can hardly be put anywhere near Milton.

When he is in the Lakes he writes, 'Perhaps this perfect country might have engendered a better poet; but we owe him [Wordsworth] much,' and then in a few weeks he returns to the same subject with 'We are the sons of Wordsworth, and after a quarter of a century which has fed us with highly spiced dainties, here we are back again with the unlearned prophet of Nature, back to our moonlight and mountain shadows, and the healing touch of Nature.' He rather fancied himself as a heretic about Shakespeare. He acknowledged freely the supremacy of Shakespeare's poetry, but he pertinaciously refused to allow an equal supremacy to the dramatist. He saw good plot structure in 'The Tempest,' 'Othello,' and 'Hamlet,' but he thought that the author of these must himself smile at those who called 'Lear' a fine play, and that he would have laughed at anyone who thought he meant to stand by such things, among others, as 'Twelfth Night' and 'Measure for Measure.' Cory's views on drama generally were, indeed, perverted by a partiality for the French theatre that amounted almost to infatuation, and when he was sixty years of age he could say, 'I firmly refuse to think Shakespeare a better playwright than Sardou.' And his obsession sweeps away the Greeks with

Shakespeare — 'Greek plays are to French plays what cold boiled veal is to snipe.' Even 'Othello' he will only allow to be 'nearly as good as it was possible for anything to be before the human mind had by evolution become capable of "Kenilworth" and "Marion de Lorme."' He was, indeed, as he claimed, *enfant du siècle*. 'It astonishes me that men do not perceive how much greater our age is than other ages.' And as for 'Kenilworth,' Scott was perhaps the writer of all others who enchained his affections most securely from first to last. 'I hold that "Heart of Midlothian" was very much more effective on the minds of Britons than all the Lake poets put together. I hold that Scott is the supreme man of letters after W. S. and before our lot, Tennyson, G. Eliot, and Currer Bell.'

These are opinions not calling for discussion, but, arbitrary as they are, stamped by personality, and in themselves suggestive of a figure that was representative of a peculiar aspect of English character. Still less do we wish to argue with him about his judgment upon writers who had a far slighter hold upon his interest either one way or the other. But, again, some of these casual impressions are worth noting. As a boy of twenty he rejoiced in Macaulay's 'Lays,' and at forty, skimming through 'Pilgrim's Progress,' he 'thought it wretched stuff and wondered Macaulay could praise it so highly.' He thought highly of George Eliot, but he did not like Goethe, and he is betrayed by Matthew Arnold's prose into the one cruel and bitter remark to be found in his correspondence. He is often dictatorial and obstinate, but on this occasion only does he offend against the ordinary canons of good taste, and the offending passage ought not to have been written, still less published.[1] He honours Spenser as being 'in the succession,' but he cannot read him 'except as I can listen to an Archdeacon's sermon. It is a task.' He thought Stevenson's 'Child's Garden of Verses' was a failure, and that Dickens had lowered the standard of writing in England, but he could 'understand insular people, with no academy to correct their taste, being bewitched by Dickens,' while 'Thackeray is not even clever, not even strong; it is all of it just the stuff, easy to understand, which one would serve up for the common idler of watering-places and parsonages in second-rate magazines.' He put George Meredith easily at the head of the later novelists. He found the 'Earthly Paradise' 'a singularly primitive, unaffected story, which gave me no head-work and very little heartache.' But when somebody gave him 'The Epic of Hades,' he merely

[1] It is fair to say that elsewhere Cory speaks of Arnold with proper respect. Instances may be found in 'Gathered Leaves,' by Mary Coleridge, 1910, where a chapter on the 'Table-Talk of William Cory' gives a pleasant account of the informal classes in Hampstead, at which Cory gave instruction in the classics to Mary Coleridge and a few other women pupils.

supposed that the young men in England did not know what a good book was since they could 'praise such stuff.' He did not like Popery and said it 'almost destroys poetry.' From the generalization he proceeds to the particular statement that in our older literature there is no good papist poet, instances Habington in support of his argument, and overlooks Southwell and Crashaw. He sometimes touched an out-of-the-way poet, and recommends to a correspondent 'a beautiful old poem, Tickell's "Elegy on Addison."' He thought that Campbell would outlive Shelley. He seldom gave expression to less particular opinions about literature; we but rarely get notes such as — 'If there is one kind of literature that I hate more than another, it is ingenious interpretation of the Bible; worse than Gladstone on Homer.'

V

His opinions on life in general are frequently full of point and admirably turned. 'I wish people would everywhere take up the pretty etiquette of presenting a guest on his departure with a nosegay. It would be much more pleasing than the sandwiches which one gets nowadays,' the humour of which is recalled by another remark that 'the lieutenants were as dull as cricketers.' His wish that 'the British monarchy would similarly pass away with Victoria' is a little unexpected from so devoted a loyalist — one who had written in his Eton days when a small boy had mocked as he was talking to a class about the Queen's marriage, 'Her Majesty is the only topic upon which I can tolerate no difference of opinion.' His mind was of the curious Tory-Liberal blend that is common in the finest English character. He was all for the State and constitution, and yet he could write half humorously, but half seriously, 'I have thought the nations would jar less and the cities would be liker to temples, if government were entrusted to young couples in their first year of wedlock. The happiness of the months just before and after marriage is perhaps an equivalent for wisdom.' Youth and death kept a constant fellowship in his mind. He exulted in the one, and was brave in contemplation of the other. 'The Universities are Highland reservoirs of spring waters gathered, the springs of youth' and then, 'Was death invented that there might be poetry. If so after all it is not so senseless an arrangement.' And he could turn with ease from the clear thinking of 'every character described by literature becomes the germs of characters and fragments of characters' to the whimsical

Other Germans . . . when not speaking of England, gave me satisfaction; and I regret more than ever that their language is indigestible. 'Herz' and 'Schmerz'

rhyme (or rime) twelve times in their version of 'Afri-
caine,' and when Vasco said, at the end of his song, 'Un-
sterblichkeit' with the South German slushing of the
guttural, it was truly nauseous.

VI

ALTHOUGH he lived to be seventy, Cory's views
and intellectual position were hardly modified after
he turned fifty, and when he died he would probably have stood by a little confession he wrote in a
letter of 1875:

> After so much tossing to and fro I cast anchor on
> Tennyson as the representative of Virgil, on France as
> the representative of Augustan Rome, on Darwin as
> wiser than Mill, on the law and the science of my own
> time, of my own nation, which gathers up and does
> justice to all the products of German penetration, on
> the synthesis of English and French thought, on re-
> publics, once more glorified by Victor Hugo and Swin-
> burne. This last is the only extravagance or vehemence,
> I think, that has any charm for me. . . .

Indeed, some years before he was fifty he seems
to have thought of himself as settled in age.

> My Eton song is finished and copied out. . . . It is a
> failure, and I must be content with prose. Too old for
> verse; the little slender vein is worked out. But I have
> my readers like better men.

But his mind never became vague, nor, except in so
far as all political thinking is beset by the curse,
was he ever given to easy generalization. The

breadth of his learning and human sympathy was always sharpened by meticulousness as to detail, even to the point of noting among much more impressive matter that he had been lecturing 'on *Is qui* with subjunctive.' It is perhaps fanciful to suppose that this habit of mind was in some way connected with his defective eyesight, but the psychological cause and effect of these things is sometimes odd in this way. When he was forty-four he notes, 'Coming back up the moor by sunset I saw, to my delight, a live bird perched on a wall, just in time with my glasses. . . . I hardly ever saw a free bird before — it was a great pleasure,' and elsewhere he speaks of the movement of a cow's forelegs as being one of the most graceful things in nature. There is something almost of insensitiveness, wholly unexpected from him, and perhaps the more so because of his own affliction, in an Egyptian travel note, when he says, 'Moreover, I wish there were not so many blinking, dull eyes. I don't mind a sprinkling of real blind folk, whose presence in the crowded lanes is a precious sign of the people's gentleness, but the amaurosis is mean and dismal.' The only other occasion where there is an ineptness of the same character in his journals, though it is in a different context altogether, is when he speaks of the Downs of Needles Bay as being 'quite as elastic and much loftier than those at Bude.' These things are trivial, but they may be noted without offence in a character that was of singular purity and sureness. In nothing, perhaps, does Cory's essential goodness — to use a somewhat discredited word in its simple meaning — show itself more sweetly than in its love of music. This was a life-long passion with him, and when it was on him he was apt to rate everything else as of little account:

Life without music is despicable, with it inexplicably strange. . . . Listening to pathetic songs I rebel against the death of those who sang them in the old times: the makers of those melodies are my unknown brethren; all others who speak in what we call words fail to let me know them thoroughly; music is the only communion of hearts, and it makes one's heart feel hopelessly empty.

In 1872 he writes in a letter:

. . . Mozart gives me the sense of perfect angelic freedom, like the best parts of our 1790–1860 poetry; like the pretty movement in 'Christabel,' in Tennyson's 'Maud,' in Keats's 'Hyperion.'

What I should like to be told is that Gluck lived to hear Mozart's best things well performed, and rejoiced in being surpassed and *fulfilled*, and to wish Virgil could hear them.

In another place he notes that 'my journals have many a bit of romance about tunes,' and as a final example of his musical enthusiasm may be given his note on the violin, which is in particular to him, he says, 'A symbol of infinity, not bounded by a keyboard, not divisible into the octaves — one can imagine it in another world, keeping its identity but endlessly extending its range and taking our ears along with it.'

Perhaps in place of a peroration it will be more fitting to take leave of our poet, himself so little rhetorical, with a story told by him with his own charm of humorous appreciation. It is an anecdote of Queen Victoria, who had apparently been doubtful about the marriage of a certain Dean and was ultimately reconciled to it. She 'joined the hands of the Dean and his lady and said to him, "Never forsake her, don't forget her, don't leave her behind on the platform."'

VII

THE following six hitherto unpublished letters, now in my possession, are given as an Appendix to this paper. They were written by Cory in January and February, 1891, less than six months before his death, to Mr. Julian Marshall, the connoisseur and collector. They have the interest of being concerned with Cory's own writings. I have attached a few explanatory notes in square brackets. Cory's idiosyncrasy in punctuation is retained.

LETTER I

[The 1877 pamphlet, 'Ionica II,' is now very scarce. When Cory gave it away 'for a shilling a copy privately,' as he puts it, he was in the habit of correcting two or three misprints. My own copy is so marked.

H. A. J. Munro, of Trinity College, Cambridge, was Kennedy Professor of Latin from 1869 to 1872.]

25 Cannon Place
N.W.
January 19 1891

Dear Sir — I send the privately printed pamphlet of 1877 which was meant originally for two or three friends and was put forth with many absurd errors due to my own carelessness — of this thing there are a good many copies in a drawer here

Of the original Ionica there are no bound copies Bain of Haymarket and Bowes of Macmillan's shop Cambridge took some few years ago all the sheets which my brother discovered in his house of which I was the tenant.

When Mr Bain told me in 1890 that he had sold his last copy and that there was a demand I with some misgivings took measures for publishing in order to save trouble or doubt to my executors.

The agent employed has had the poor booklet badly printed, and I myself was careless in looking at the proofs

My friends have pointed out to me 'tyrranous' and croppres — (croppies) and I have observed (besides heart for art) 'doubt' for 'doat' on p 184 l 10

I daresay there are other slips

As you say you are curious about obscure books I venture to say that there is an obscure schoolbook Lucretilis published by Ingalton Drake of Eton College which was in writing declared by the late leader of English Latinists H. A. J. Munro to be the *only* good imitation of Horace The 'Key' to this schoolbook gives my Latin and I, who am no judge, like that Latin well enough to read it I tried to imitate Horace in a scrap about Britomart and I have printed in magazines seven or eight sets of 'Rhymes after Horace'

I am yours faithfully
Wm. Cory

Letter II

[The Rhymes after Horace to which Cory refers in these letters do not seem to have been recovered from the magazines. Reference to the files of Murray's and Macmillan's of that time show that his contributions were as follows: Murray's: October, 1889, 'Licymnia' (Hor. Od. II, 12); December, 1889, 'Achilles' (Hor. Epod. XIII). Macmillan's: August, 1888, 'Rhymes after Horace,' 'Neæra' (Hor. Epod. xv), 'Asterie' (Hor. Od. III, 7); September, 1889, 'Rhymes after Horace,' 'Phyllis I' (Hor. Od. II, 4), 'II' (Hor. Od. IV, 11). These were variously attributed to the author of 'Ionica,' 'Ofella,' and 'Ofellus.'

Cory was always emphatic from the first that his poem should not have won the Chancellor's medal in competition with Maine's.]

Jan. 20 1891

Dear Sir — Mr. Ingalton Drake Publisher Eton College Windsor probably has copies of the Key to Lucretilis at 2/ a piece and will sell one to anyone but an Eton schoolboy — he would recognise my name — You would hardly care for the English translations which was/ is used by boys learning how to make 'Lyrics.' I think this costs 2/ I should never have attached any value to the booklet but for Munro's surprising letter — he gave me as a reward a copy of his Horace which I always use in Lessons (gratis lessons) with ladies

The Magazines to which I sent my rhymes after Horace were Murray's and Macmillan's in 1888 or 1889 — I kept for myself only manuscript copies some of which are in a book first employed in the keeping of Calverley's Soracte Bandusia Leuconoe etc

The things I sent to the Magazine were Asterie Neæra* Phyllis (ne sit ancillæ) Phyllis Est mihi nonum Licymnia. I did not send a 'Donec Gratus Eram' which I did long ago at the request of a Newnham lady nor Barine (C J Foxs favourite Ode) which being now

* Epodes.

printed is by a well read Cambridge man taken to be a tribute to a *Russian* lady of fast habits

Amongst the things kept back I have a 40 line thing in blank verse which I made for a literary lady — her father showed it to Lord Tennyson — it is a translation of a bit of Euripides Supplices giving five characters of slain warriors. I sent through a Cambridge friend to a Cambridge Magazine about 18 months ago a bit of Æneid the March of Camilla in blank verse done like other things in usum virginum

Dr Whewell was very courteous to me in 1843 when he gave the imprimatur to my Plato which got the medal that was really due to a beautiful precious *poem* of Maine's I often show Maine's, my own never.

I am yours gratefully

Wm Cory

I treat 'Ionica II' as waste paper. I cant imagine it sold by itself.

Letter III

[Cecil Spring-Rice was Sir Cecil Arthur Spring-Rice, who died in 1918 and was latterly British Ambassador at Washington. The voyage referred to was during Cory's Egyptian travels with the Countess of Winchelsea and her sons. The ship was the 'Ceylon,' and Cory in his Journal gives a graphic account of a storm in the Bay of Biscay, when the behaviour of the Captain (Evans) provoked his unbounded admiration. A Captain Rice is also spoken of.]

25 Cannon Place,
N.W.
February 7 1891

My Dear Sir, — I have found Macmillan's Magazine September 1889 — its cover states that it contains Rhymes after Horace by Ofellus, but I have long ago

torn out the pages thus indicated and given them to
someone — I believe they were Asterie and Neæra *i.e.*
Quid fles Asterie   and Nox erat et cœlo

I retain them in my own writing in an old copybook,
and if you like I can lend you the copybook The then
Editor of Macmillan's Magazine   Mowbray Morris was
formerly in my class at Eton *not my pupil* he preserved
his anonymity with a stately recognition of my identity
and I rank him in my curiosities of literature. The
Editor of Murray, now a publisher, was my pupil for a
short time. Neither of these potentates expressed a wish
for continuance of my tribute

I should never have attempted rhyming after Horace
had I not been asked by my pupil Eva Hugessen to try
'Donec Gratus' which she had tried

I imagine you are akin to another pupil of mine Cecil
Spring Rice whom I knew as a little boy and have heard
of since he grew up — In January 1873 I was on board
ship with a kinsman of his, a Marshall who had been at
Eton with me though junior to me — with him I had
pleasant chats in the Mediterranean

I venture to offer you, as you deign to take interest in
my things, the loan of my copy of Lucretilis as it has
short notes as to the origin of some of the things — I am
more egotistical about that humble schoolbook than
about anything else — at least I have a sneaking wish
that it may escape the fate of my other things and last
a little longer.

As to Plato I am a mere dabbler but I have helped
several women in Phædo, Apologia, Phædrus, Georgias,
Symposium, Theætetus

I remain yours very truly

WM CORY

Letter IV

[The autograph 'Pour Rire' is as follows. It is written by Cory, as was his custom, without punctuation, the spaces being left to denote pauses, and it is so printed here.

Pour Rire

Mat Prior   diplomat and wit
In Paris   in the Opera pit
next to a Marquis chanced to sit
Well sang the tenor   and the lord
hummed   as he fancied   in accord
and by the humming Mat was bored.
Between two acts the ape would chat
So turning   and accosting Mat
he said   'a splendid tenor that'
Mat would not give the man his due.
'damn him.' 'Why damn him?' 'O Moseu
'he sings so loud I can't hear you.'

With this is a Limerick which is hardly worth printing.]

February 6   1891

My Dear Sir — I send by post a little copy book started first for Calverley — it contains rough copies of the 2 Phyllis that went to McMillan, and other scraps

I add an autograph pour rire   There are — naturally — sundries in my copybooks and flyleaves — some things have perished   My heir will probably not care for what I wish to save, sundry bits of Greek turned from English

I am proud of having been, long ago so lucky as to do a bit of Latin which went into a schoolbook that I have never even seen, called folia silvulæ or silvulæfoliorum or both — 'reviewed' in a paper — my scrap was I believe quoted — so it was seen by Tennyson, and in his autograph I saw that he called my version of his 'Hesper' *exquisite.* So I valued *that* scrap at least (principibus placuisse)

I am

Yours very truly

Wm Cory

LETTER V

25 Cannon Place
    N.W.

['Gemini and Virgo,' one of Calverley's most celebrated pieces, appeared in 'Verses and Translations,' first published in 1862. William George Clarke, joint editor of the Cambridge Shakespeare, was Public Orator at Cambridge from 1857 to 1870, and endowed the Clarke Lectureship in English Literature at Trinity.]

February 16   (1891)

My Dear Sir — The parcel containing my two relics and the four valuable volumes that you give me arrived just now and caught me at home.

I have been away and shall be again

I have in former years bought to give away some Calverley, and borrowed other Calverley, and I have known enough of him to enable me to think of him and sometimes talk of him. I shall be glad to go all through the four volumes and I hope I may live to read Theocritus once more — with ladies — under his guidance.

My wife tells me that I very seldom smile but I know that I laugh often, and laugh heartily *when alone.* This is a guarantee against madness.

Gemini and Virgo amused many a boy in my little room a quarter of a century ago.

The last Calverleys that I copied were in a recent Cambridge collection of merry rhymes of which I forget the title, and I thought of the author when I was in Cambridge last July. The wit of *my* Cambridge in the

early forties was W. G. Clarke, he got the prize in our
'Epigram Club' with a poem infinitely too long to be
called an epigram. About a Proctor chased by his own
bulldogs.

Rendering hearty thanks for your gift I remain   dear
Sir

Yours sincerely
Wm Cory

Letter VI

[Calverley's 'Fly Leaves' was first published in 1872. 'The Back-
Slider and Other Poems,' by Antæus, was published in 1890, and is by
a poet who is less known than he should be — W. J. Ibbett. Frankland
Lushington was probably Franklin Lushington, Accountant-General
of Madras, who published some martial verses, 'Points of War' in
1855. The note from Richard Burton, enclosed by Cory, is as follows:

Reid's Jan. 4

Dear Sir, — With great pleasure on Saturday — if possible.
Please remind Madame of the Carne [?] e altro. Many thanks for the
loan of the book. I have only dipped into it. Before Franschio's day
electricity was used at the Castle of [?] near Trieste and V. Hugo
mentions this in the 'Travailleurs de la Mer.'

I am dear Sir
Very truly yours
R. F. Burton.]

William Cory, Esq.

In 1881 Cory had written from Madeira to Lord Esher: 'Madame
(his wife) is quite a Calypso to the R.N. captains, and her last conquest
is that real Ulysses, Captain Burton, the Mahommedan, would-be
Mormon, etc.'

February 23 1891

Dear Sir, — Yes. I duly received the two things returned by you. I have been feasting on Flyleaves with
more wonder than ever. I perceive that I once had the
honour of being in a volume with Calverley. He was

asked, it seems by Mont. Butler to translate into verse
(Latin) as I into Greek verse Lord Carlisle's lines
about Lady St. German's tree — the tiny thing is called
'Flebilis Arbor' I think I never read such good biographical writing as Seeley's reminiscences of Calverley

Some anonymous poet has sent to anonymous me
through Geo. Allen, a libellus of 20 pages called 'Back-
slider' by Antæous, printed (100 copies) for the author
sold by Elkin Mathews Vigo Street W They are more
interesting to me than the lately lent volumes of Robert
Bridges and Mrs Woods, but far less than Sir Alfred
Lyall's.

'To a dead Mistress' seems to me original and clever,
and it might have been printed in a magazine

A friend of mine seems to have resumed an old project that he and I made long ago, to print a set of poems
of all sorts of writers for barrack libraries under the title
Sabretasch and I have just tried to remember the things
about soldiership that I have read Amongst these are
two written by my Cambridge friend Frankland Lushington who was in [word illegible] and perhaps still is —
to my disgust his 'Cabul' did not get the Chancellor's
medal

I am dear Sir

Yours sincerely

WM. CORY

Would you like to have a note written by Sir Richard
Burton, he was worth seeing . . . ten years ago

LORD DE TABLEY [1]

JOHN BYRNE, LEICESTER WARREN, who became
Lord de Tabley in 1887, was born in 1835 and died
in 1895. His first volume of poems appeared in
1859, and he was publishing until the time of his
death. His period was, therefore, Victorian without qualification, and no stranger coming to his
work with a knowledge of English poetry could fail
to recognize in it clear marks of the age of Tennyson
and Browning and Morris and Swinburne and
Arnold. His reputation has never been, nor is it
ever likely to be, with theirs. His mastery of the
muse was far too inconstant a thing to give him
place in the forefront of an age, but, at his best, he
was not merely a small poet imitating these greater
ones with talent, but an authentic maker drawing
his variable inspiration from the same sources that
worked in the masters of the time to an ampler
though not always a richer gathering.

In the case of the foremost men it is, when all is
said, idle to dispute whether one age is greater than
another in poetry. Milton, Pope, Wordsworth,
Tennyson, for example — you may like one better
than another, and have very good reasons for your

[1] Prefixed to *Select Poems of Lord de Tabley*. (Humphrey Milford,
1924.)

liking, but that is about all there is to be said in this matter of degree. The great poets have this in common, that most of the time their work, so to speak, comes off. To follow these four instances, in spite of a great deal of nonsense that is talked about Wordsworth by people who do not read him, and, for that matter, about the other three as well, no one who really cares for poetry, and patiently gives himself to the understanding of a poet like any of these four, seriously wishes any considerable volume of his work away. One is not talking of the *dilettante* readers in poetry, who have a perfectly legitimate taste merely for a lyric here and there, but of those others who believe that in the poetic canon of their race is to be found at once the most interesting and inspiring expression of that race's spirit. The great poet's life is always and stead-fastly preoccupied with his poetry, and when a man like Milton set about writing a poem it was found more likely than not to be a good one, and, if the reader does not see it, it is, at least, as likely as not that Milton is right and he is wrong. So that, again to speak of these four, we shall find that each of them brought all the resources of a rich and powerful nature to the accomplishment of a great life's aim in poetry, and that each of them suc-ceeded. That Tennyson's particular kind of verse was not Pope's, nor Pope's Milton's, does not matter. In each case the great work was done and

the account closed. We may call Milton a greater
poet than Tennyson if we like, but Milton would
laugh at us.

When, however, we come to the smaller men the
case is altered. The difference between a poet like
de Tabley, for example, and a poet like Tennyson
is not that Tennyson reaches an excellence altogether beyond de Tabley's range, but that Tennyson does it twenty times for de Tabley's once, and
that, moreover, at one sitting, as it were, Tennyson
will do it consistently and de Tabley but fitfully.
Inspiration remains the best word, and inspiration
is common in the one case and very occasional in
the other. The result is that, now to particularize,
in de Tabley's 'Collected Poems,' which fill five
hundred closely printed pages in small type, there
is an immense amount of waste tissue, and a public
that can only know him through such a volume is
little likely to have the patience to know him at all.
This is an injustice to a poetic gift about which,
when the tide was moving, there can be no question whatever. Critical opinion at the moment is
rather at outs with even the Swinburnes and the
Morrises and the Tennysons themselves, and
possibly it may be even less ready to reconsider the
claims of a lesser light from the firmament in which
these were the stars of greater magnitude. Critical
opinion of the moment about things of a moment
ago, however, has a way of being very soon found

out, and this selection is put forward in the belief that less fashionable and more permanent judgment will be glad always to have the best of a poet who, for all his defects, could be very good indeed.

De Tabley belonged to an age in which the defects of its poetry were peculiarly troublesome. There are times when the poets even when they are not writing at their best do not necessarily write quite tediously. The elaborate and profuse vigour and sweetness of the Elizabethans may sometimes fall into an almost ludicrous disorder, but at their worst they still have the touch of divinity upon them. After Donne the poetry of the seventeenth century, varied as it was, has, nevertheless, for its governing characteristic that quality which has given it the term 'metaphysical.' That in its play of intellectual wit it disregarded the deeper things of passion is a belief obviously untenable by the witness of such names as Marvell and Vaughan and Crashaw and Herbert and Herrick, to say nothing of Milton or of a dozen other known, and many hardly known, names. But there was in the work of all that age a certain simple fundamental quality of brain that seemed to save almost the smallest talent, no matter into what fantastic excesses it might fall, from mere dullness. One can read through volume after volume of forgotten verse books of the time and pass from admiration to every kind of reaction but boredom. There is, for example, but a poor little penn'orth of fame in the great world for the score or so of Professor Saintsbury's Caroline Poets put together, but to care for poetry is, I think, to find scarcely one page too many in the nearly two thousand of that masterly piece of devoted scholarship and taste. The seventeenth century could do silly and even false things with its wits, but the wits were always there. A poet then, in his bad moments, could betray himself into saying that the light of his dead mistress's eyes would dim all the lights of heaven, or into any other kind of extravagance, but, although he has no answer to the charge of not believing what he says, he can nearly always, at least, plead mastery of his conceit. The obvious defect in the lower levels of metaphysical poetry in the seventeenth century is a lack of emotional sincerity, but there is hardly ever a complete failure in intellectual interest. When Dryden and Reason set out to correct this highfalutin of the mind they did much to doctor a manifest disease, but their preoccupation led them too much into making poetry commonsensical and the forgetting of such glories as

> 'The grave's a fine and private place
> But none I think do there embrace.'

and in their poorer work they showed that common-sense in its lassitudes could be perhaps more reasonable, but certainly far duller, than the lapses of intellectual passion, and poetry very often found itself reasoned out of existence. Then came the romantic revival, standing first and foremost for a passionate emotional sincerity such as had hardly characterized English poetry before. Not even in the greatest days of the sixteenth century had the poets so poignantly and uncompromisingly laid bare the very trouble of their souls. This is why many people, to whom what are perhaps some of the rarest delights of poetry are unknown, find in the work of those men from Blake, or more probably Wordsworth, to Keats, a consolation that they do not know in the poetry of any other age. This intimate, human, troubled quality added, we know how richly, to the best of our English glories, but it, too, had the inevitable other side to its account. The emotional sincerity knocked the conceit in both senses out of poetry as it had come from the seventeenth century and, more profitably perhaps, it put the reason of that later time in its proper place. But it had its own dangers.

It was not possible for a poet of any consequence at all, working under this new impulse, to fall into the intellectual posturings that seduced even the finer men of an earlier age in their unwary moments. Love poetry, for example, from Blake onwards has quite simply a new and deeper sincerity than had marked the volume of it for generations.

But this emotional abandon, this fearless wearing
of the heart upon the sleeve, while it was duly con-
trolled by intellectual power by all the poets at
their best, was too concerned with its own passion
to pay any great heed, for its own sake, to the exercise of wit that had always been a chief characteristic of the metaphysicals. And this meant that,
when the pressure was relaxed, a quality which
had so well served the less urgent moods of poetry
was no longer there for service, and the poets fell
into a habit of merely repeating very dirly their
own imaginative utterance at times when the imagination was not in play. The result was a serious
one, and finally exemplified in the case of Swinburne, of whom it has been observed often enough
that his quite inferior work is at first glance so like
his very finest as to be almost indistinguishable
from it. The trouble was apparent even in the
earlier stages of the new movement. It is to be
found often in Byron, even Shelley is not wholly
free from it, while Wordsworth and Keats had their
moments of hesitation. As the so-called, and on
the whole well-called, romanticism became more
self-conscious with the growing of the nineteenth
century, the danger became more and more per-
vasive, and, while it was the chief disability with
which even so great a genius as that of Swinburne
had to contend, it has, I think, more than anything else made for the obscuring of reputations

like that of de Tabley's altogether. I think this little volume should put de Tabley's poetic endowment beyond question. But in reading through his collected work one is continually finding passages which, while they have an almost bewildering outward resemblance to some of the best things that he wrote, are unsatisfactory, even at a first reading, and on a second assert themselves as having been written merely out of an expert habit when inspiration was asleep. It is then that the world of crumbling cliffs and pale blossoms, of which de Tabley could write so poignantly and truly when poetry was alert in him, becomes merely tiresome, and minor in the really bad sense.

In making this selection the first thing, obviously, was to give a representative showing of de Tabley's lyrical poems. This I have done to the best of my judgment. There remained the longer pieces, which presented some difficulty. Those people who cannot read poetry at all unless it is in short lyric form miss many delights, and it is, by the way, interesting to note that a good many poets of our time are again beginning to write long poems. It is one thing for a poet to make what should be a short poem into a long one, as de Tabley often did, and quite another to have a taste for such poetic concepts only as can be put into a little space. But while the reader who shies at a long poem is, perhaps, rather more in need of a holiday of some sort

than anything else, he cannot be disregarded and
he is as likely to refuse a poem of two hundred lines
as one of two thousand. It so happens that what
seems to me to be by far de Tabley's finest achievement is also nearly his longest one ('Orestes' is a
few lines longer). And in the belief that any reader
who cares for the longer 'rests,' to borrow a term
from tennis, will turn to this as readily as to a
series of shorter long pieces, I have decided to let
this alone stand with the lyrics. And any reader
who approaches 'Philoctetes' with that leisure and
submissiveness which every sustained work of art
demands will be very richly rewarded. For it is
here, with a subject wholly suited to elaborate
treatment, that all de Tabley's powers combined
to one wholly satisfying result. The neo-classical
drama of the nineteenth century has many riches
but, even remembering 'Atalanta,' I do not think
that any is rarer than this. The form suited de
Tabley's instinct exactly, and yet, far from con-
straining the humanity in him, it enriched it.
'Philoctetes' is not only the most moving poem
that de Tabley wrote, it is, attentively read, one of
the most moving long poems of the century. The
description of the death of Heracles, the meditation
beginning 'Spirit of man, to whom these petty
stings,' the tenderness of the scenes with Ægle,
the clear-sighted drama of the conflict between
Philoctetes and Ulysses and Pyrrhus, and the

magnificent speech in which the hero sums up the whole matter and takes farewell of the Lemnian peasants, are all conceived and shaped in the manner of great poetry. The characterization throughout, moreover, is exact and admirable, and through the whole work runs a thread of pure lyric beauty which is most memorable, perhaps, in the lovely figure of Pan given in the last part of the Chorus beginning 'In wonder and time-mists.' With such a poem to his credit, de Tabley cannot but be secure against long neglect.

WILLIAM ERNEST HENLEY [1]

SPEAKING of Byron, Henley says that he 'was not interested in words and phrases, but in the greater truths of destiny and emotion. His empire is over the imagination and the passions.' As a critical judgment this is far less shrewd than was common with Henley, but it is suggestive in relation to his own work as a poet. Henley was a remarkable figure in the literary world of his day, moving in no scholarly seclusion, but coming out into the open field of journalism, and bearing himself always with spirit and dignity. The best of his work is a durable contribution to the finest kind of popular criticism, vivid, far from unlearned, in close touch with the ordinary and confused affairs of life. On any given subject he might have to yield at points to the specialist, but few men have covered so wide a range with so warm an understanding and with a mind so well versed in the evidence of the case. It is as a critic that he will be remembered, and it is of his critical work that there is most to be said. But he produced a good deal of creative work, and, in common with most writers who work in both kinds, he no doubt hoped that it was in this that he

[1] *The Works of William Ernest Henley.* Five volumes, Macmillan, 1920–21.

came to his best achievement. So that, although on the whole it seems likely that this side of his expression will be the first to fade, it cannot be passed by without consideration.

'He was not interested in words and phrases, but in the greater truths of destiny and emotion.' This, in the last analysis, is true of Henley as a poet. He would have accepted the judgment with pride; and that he would have done so is indicative of his real weakness. When he adds that Byron's empire was over the imagination and the passions, he says more than justly can be put in for himself. Henley's poetic world was not that of passion and imagination, but that of clear-sighted morality, which was sometimes transfigured by indignation. It was in this world that he moved as a master in a great deal of his critical work. But it was a world that was, as it always must be, incomplete as an environment for rich poetic creation. In passing, it may be remarked that it merely is not true to say of Byron that in his great poetic moods, of which for all his failures he had as many as most poets, he was not interested in words and phrases. Byron knew, as in practice Henley did not, that, while it is passion and imagination that must condition the poetic faculty, the only possible consummation of that faculty comes through the most exact and disciplined ordering of words and phrases.

Henley brought to his poetry many beautiful

qualities. He had real courage, he had a great-hearted tenderness, he hated Pecksniffs and impure Puritans; he was, in short, a very chivalrous man, with rare intellectual gifts. But he did not perceive that merely to be these things, while it might do anything else for you, could not make you into a poet. Every now and again this fine moral impetus in his being would move with such force as to achieve something which remains memorable and beyond the reach of any but poets of the most indisputable magic. Such pieces as 'Matri Dilectissimœ' and 'On the Way to Kew,' and the well-known 'Out of the night that covers me,' and 'Or ever the knightly years were gone,' are good things for any man to have written. Coming from the finer airs of Herrick or Marvell or Keats, our minds may not often go to Henley, but at other times we find ourselves recalling,

> 'Out of the night that covers me,
>   Black as the Pit from pole to pole,
> I thank whatever gods may be
>   For my unconquerable soul ...'

or

> 'Or ever the knightly years were gone
>   With the old world to the grave,
> I was a King in Babylon
>   And you were a Christian Slave ...'

and we do so with a pleasure that we do not question. But Henley very rarely came to this excellence in his verse. The great body of it suffers from the fatal defect of having been subjected to no emotional selection, a defect which Henley very thoroughly understood when considering the work of other men. The sequence of Hospital sketches, for example, is no more than brilliant journalism. Brilliant journalism in its place is all very well; and, when a man aiming at it accomplishes it, all credit is due to him, but you cannot pass it off as poetry. These poems, one feels all the time as one reads them, are as much an accident as the occasion of Henley's being in the hospital at all. It is no case of carefully selected emotion being projected through an occasion that shall give it final form, as it seems to the poet; it is, rather, a vivid observation catching up this, that, and the other fragment of casual event and setting it down, not with imaginative but merely graphic power. The tranquillity which, as Wordsworth pointed out, is the condition in which emotion must be recollected for the creation of poetry, is precisely the condition in which the poet works with the utmost precision in that matter of words and phrases. And in most of Henley's verse there is unmistakable evidence that he was working, not in tranquillity, but in Fleet Street.

'We flash across the level,
　　We thunder thro' the bridges,
We bicker down the cuttings,
　　We sway along the ridges.'

This is not an unfair example of a prevalent quality in Henley's verse; and it does not begin to exist as poetry.

On the whole, the volume of Poems, running to nearly three hundred pages, is the one of the five forming the admirable collected edition now published that is least likely to serve Henley's memory. He was a skilled writer always and handled many verse forms with ease, but only very rarely in any of them does he come to that last continence which is style. It is interesting to note that he often writes in a manner which is to-day supposed to be very revolutionary, but he seems to have done it without theories, merely because it was easy.

> 'The stalwart Ships,
> The beautiful and bold adventurers!
> Stationed out yonder in the isle,
> The tall Policeman,
> Flashing his bull's-eye, as he peers
> About him in the ancient vacancy,
> Tells them this way is safety — this way home.'

That might pass without question in to-morrow morning's anthology, and be held to show how unnecessary the great English metrical forms had become to progressive genius. The Henley of this kind, however, is already forgotten, but poetry will always have a secure, if modest, place for such forthright excellence as this:

> Some starlit garden gray with dew,
> Some chamber flushed with wine and fire,

What matters where, so I and you
    Are worthy our desire?

Behind, a past that scolds and jeers
For ungirt loins and lamps unlit;
In front, the unmanageable years,
    The trap upon the Pit.

Think on the shame of dreams for deeds,
The scandal of unnatural strife,
The slur upon immortal needs,
    The treason done to life.

Arise! no more a living lie,
And with me quicken and control
Some memory that shall magnify
    The universal Soul.

There is just a little sheaf of this quality to be garnered from Henley's poems, and he is a fortunate man who can contribute even so much to so great an inheritance.

Before passing to Henley the critic, a word must be said of the four plays that he wrote in collaboration with Stevenson. In these there are passages of patent merit. The Stevenson of 'Treasure Island' could not fail in the course of a long work to find moments of enchantment, flushed with the true broadside manner, and coloured of the best. And, given the situation right and the characters really agog, Henley had a gift of dramatic dialogue — if it was Henley's, as I suspect — that could firmly hold the stage for five minutes at a stretch. But these things do not make drama; and, as dramas, these four plays are the merest exercises, and very poor ones at that. It is incredible that two writers of such outstanding ability could at times become so jejune. It is all very well for men of genius to have larks, but even in their larks there must be some conscience, and if there is any conscience in these plays I do not discover it. 'Admiral Guinea' has scenes of the true Stevensonian glamour, but it has nothing else of the smallest dramatic truth. 'Robert Macaire' is a very elaborate joke, which certainly does not come off in reading any more than I can believe it to come off on the stage. 'Beau Austin,' although it has perhaps the best three minutes to be found in any of the plays, is no more than Sheridan-Goldsmith pastiche. And 'Deacon Brodie' succeeds only in making villainy appear more imbecile than virtue. It is in this play, too, that we have the most hilarious examples of the abuse of soliloquy. Henley in his article on 'Othello' speaks of soliloquy as 'an expedient in dramatic art abominable to the play-going mind.' In that essay he is inclined to accept the device because of Shakespeare's use of it, not seeing that in its proper function it may be a magnificent element in great dramatic form. But that a critic who could raise the question at all should put his name to a play in which over and over again one of the characters speaks like this,

Now for one of the Deacon's headaches! Rogues all, rogues all! (*Goes to clothes-press, and proceeds to change his coat.*) On with the new coat and into the new life! Down with the Deacon and up with the robber!... Only the stars to see me! (*Addressing the bed.*) Lie there, Deacon! sleep and be well to-morrow. As for me, I'm a man once more till morning. (*Gets out of the window.*)

leaves one, as they say in the ring, guessing. They just won't do, and that is all there is to be said of the plays. But to leave them with the mind on that short scene in 'Beau Austin,' which is perhaps the best thing to be found in them, let me quote. Austin, it may be remembered, first at Fenwick's persuasion but now from genuine impulse, is about to present his addresses to Barbara, who has been one of his conquests. The lady's young brother, Anthony, a cornet who has neither brains nor morals, conceives it to be his duty to shoot or beat the Beau.

Barbara. Mr. Austin. (*She shows Austin in, and retires.*)

Austin. You will do me the justice to acknowledge, Mr. Fenwick, that I have been not long delayed by my devotion to the Graces.

Anthony. So, sir, I find you in my house —

Austin. And charmed to meet you again. It went against my conscience to separate so soon. Youth, Mr. Musgrave, is to us older men a perpetual refreshment.

Anthony. You came here, sir, I suppose, upon some errand?

Austin. My errand, Mr. Musgrave, is to your fair sister. Beauty, as you know, comes before valour.

Anthony. In my own house, and about my own sister, I presume I have the right to ask for something more explicit.

Austin. The right, my dear sir, is beyond question; but it is one, as you were going on to observe, on which no gentleman insists.

Fenwick. Anthony, my good fellow, I think we had better go.

Anthony. I have asked a question.

Austin. Which I was charmed to answer, but which, on repetition, might begin to grow distasteful.

Anthony. In my own house —

Fenwick. For God's sake, Anthony!

Austin. In your aunt's house, young gentleman, I shall be careful to refrain from criticism. I am come upon a visit to a lady: that visit I shall pay; when you desire (if it be possible that you desire it) to resume this singular conversation, select some fitter place. Mr. Fenwick, this afternoon, may I present you to his Royal Highness?

Anthony. Why, sir, I believe you must have misconceived me. I have no wish to offend: at least at present.

Austin. Enough, sir. I was persuaded I had heard amiss. I trust we will be friends.

Fenwick. Come, Anthony, come! here is your sister.

Henley, the critic, is another matter altogether. It may sometimes be charged against him that he was superficial, and, in a way, justly. But it was a superficiality which Henley himself would have been at no pains to disown, since what is meant is not that he did not feel profoundly, but that his interests were chiefly along the highways of critical thought and creative effort, and that he was not much concerned with the remoter things of speculation nor with the rarer and more elusive kind of personality. The result is that a few readers will find Henley's pronouncement altogether shallow and ill-considered, in the case of a writer such as Landor, for example. That imperturbable spirit, casting the imagination and passion, of which Henley speaks, into a form so austere, so little conscious of the world's judgment, so sufficient to itself, seemed to so plain and blunt a mind as Henley's to be 'not only inferior in kind but poverty-stricken in degree,' and its creative faculty to be 'limited by the reflexion that its one achievement is Landor.' This is to be superficial with a vengeance; and the fortunate thing is that Henley very rarely turned his attention at all to subjects of which he had so little understanding. It is in such studies as those of Fielding, Burns, and the motley that made up Byron's world, that Henley is at his best, not only as a critic but as a writer altogether.

The outstanding quality of all Henley's work in this his best kind is a moral courage of a particular strain which we to-day, taught by a generation of writers who in this at least have learnt wisdom, may find less unusual than it was, say, in 1896, when the Burns essay was first published. Twenty-

five years ago it was not difficult for a man to
speak his mind about life; but, if he spoke with
courage and independence, he was apt to find
acceptance only among a small body of artists and
thinkers. Thirty years had passed, it is true, since
Swinburne sent the larger public into convulsions
by 'Poems and Ballads,' but even after that lapse
of time such a book would have been greeted with
a considerable, if not an equal, storm of protest.
To-day, however much it might flutter a few
hearts, 'Poems and Ballads' would at least leave
the moral sense of the public unshocked. And that
this is so is largely due to writers, of whom Henley
was by no means the least, who came out into the
open and challenged, not a coterie but what is
known as public opinion, with the declaration that
nearly all moral judgments are immoral and that
what really matters is not points of view but life.

In reading his essay on Burns, one is reminded
of the teaching and practice of the truest worldly
philosopher who ever lived, Christ. It is strange
that so clear-sighted and lucid a moralist as the
founder of Christianity should so often be advanced in support of a dullness of spirit that was
the constant mark of his reproof. The people who
said it against him that he consorted with publicans
and sinners were at least intelligible, and stood for
a definite, if bad, morality. There are a great many
people in the world who do not like publicans and

sinners, who think that they themselves are better than publicans and sinners, and that some kind of outlawry is the desert of such as these. It is a most lamentable state of the human mind, but at least it asserts itself plainly, deceiving itself as to what is right but not as to what it thinks. The astonishing moralists are those who tell you that Christ consorted with publicans and sinners, as though it were a peculiar and crowning virtue in him; that so good a man should have stooped to the company of these forlorn people seems to them to be witness of the most exemplary holiness. The thing that this kind of mind always overlooks is that Christ himself never thought of these people as publicans and sinners at all; and that he would have rated in no uncertain terms the spiritual ignorance that supposes that he could have thought it any kind of virtue to foregather with people whom he merely saw as men and women a little more entangled by circumstance than others, and consequently needing an even tenderer understanding.

It is this Christlike spirit that informs such essays as these of Henley on Fielding and Burns. Here was a critic who not only had his fine sense of literary excellence, but brought a real ethical standard to his appraising of it, a standard that recognized first and last that self-righteousness and morality cannot live together. The result is that in the study of Burns, for example, we have the whole of the man quite fearlessly set down — unstable, betrayed by circumstance into all sorts of follies and even worse, often enough spiritually thriftless, descending at times to the level of a mean antagonist, and, with it all, magnificent. Henley sees these defects in his hero, and is no more afraid of them than Burns himself was at pains to conceal them. He passes no moral judgment on them, since moral judgment is not his business. He merely perceives them, vividly, as part of a character, moving in its other scale to a courage, a generosity, and a passionate charity such as have never been excelled in any human heart. And this complete Burns is for Henley life, something to contemplate with all one's understanding and humility, something so much more marvellous in itself than it can be in the testing by preconceived standards.

Henley was, in fact, a good man, and like most good men said much that is shocking to the respectable ones. Also his goodness, as usual, expressed itself often with a very natural gaiety, which nowhere shows itself to better advantage than in the brilliant character-sketches which make up the chapter called 'Byron's World.' Nothing could be more spirited in its kind than the little study of Gentleman Jackson, Byron's great prize-fighting friend, of whom the poet said, when some one suggested that this was no company for him to keep, 'Jackson's manners are infinitely superior to those of the fellows of my college whom I meet at the high table.' Jackson repaid the admiration in full, saying of Byron that nobody could be more fearless, and that he showed great courage always 'in coming up to the blows.' It is, again, the life that takes Henley's mood, the life of an age, as he says,

dreadful no doubt; for all its solid foundations, of faith and dogma in the Church and of virtue and solvency in the State, a fierce, drunken, gambling, 'keeping,' adulterous, high-living, hard-drinking, hard-hitting, brutal age. But it was Byron's; and 'Don Juan' and the 'Giaour' are as naturally its outcomes as 'Absalom and Achitophel' is an expression of the Restoration, and 'In Memoriam' a product of Victorian England.

Even when Henley makes his sympathy clear, as in the case of Byron against 'Pippin,' Lady Byron, he still sees all round his question.

On January 8, 1816, Pippin has asked Dr Baillie, 'as a friend,' to tell her whether Byron is or is not mad; a week after she leaves Piccadilly Terrace for Kirkby Mallory, her father's residence; next day, 'by medical advice,' she writes cheerfully and affectionately to her husband; and that is all. They never met again; and the next that Duck (Byron) knew of Pippin was that she had taken his child from him, and purposed — strongly purposed — that he should never more set eyes on either of them. He never did. Byron the poet, Byron the dandy, Byron the *homme à femmes*, Byron the lover, Byron the husband and father — the little country blue-stocking

was more than a match for them. Against them all she
set her unaided wits, and against them all she scored;
and scored so heavily that in France, and places where
they know better, the name and fame of the British
Female suffer for Pippin's achievement yet.

This human quality in Henley's work would, it
need hardly be said, not suffice in itself to make him
the critic he is. It is, rather, that, when this nature
in him is stirred, his critical faculty becomes alert
also, and he discovers an authoritative sense of
literary values. When, as in the case of Landor,
the emotion of his subject escapes him, the expression of that emotion naturally enough seems
to him to be in itself something inadequate. And all
that can be said about it, as in every case of æsthetic appreciation, is that, so far as Henley's mind
was concerned, the expression was inadequate.
Landor remains, and Henley proves his worth
elsewhere, and little harm is done. In the 'Fielding'
and 'Burns,' on the other hand (one returns to
these essays since, on the whole, they stand as the
best of Henley's achievement), his personal sympathy with the life of his subject finds the nicest
modulation in the analysis that he makes of the
form in which that life found expression. And
these papers are full not only of human understanding but of critical wisdom. We have not only warm-
hearted persuasion, but a very rare insight into the
processes of literary art. This, for example, of

Fielding, is perfect in its discrimination and embodies a general principle that inferior criticism always overlooks:

... he has ever a kindly, and at the same time a leisurely, half-laughing, half-reticent mastery of his creation, which he never permits to get out of hand; so that he is able, on occasion, to assert, and to make us assent to, such an outrageous familiarity as that of the boxing of Squire Western's ears, by a person unnamed, whose sole title to credence is that, being an officer and a gentleman, he is as well acquainted with Squire Western as Squire Western's creator. That is to say, a great deal better than Sir Walter Scott and Mr. Saintsbury. Sir Walter thought that Mr. Western ought to have retaliated; Mr. Saintsbury (speaking, he says, as a Tory) agrees, and seems to think this inimitable and daring touch the Novelist's 'one slip.' For myself, I am, like Mr. Dobson, of Mr. Fielding's party; for the reason that he knew his Western, and that his Western, if we are to accept him at all, must be accepted on his terms.

And so it is always when he is in touch with his subject. He may sometimes be deceived by a manner as to what lies behind. To the example of Landor might be added that of Philip Sidney, in whom Henley could see only affectation and conceit, and in whom he only permitted himself vaguely to suspect that there was a heart beating under 'the buckram and broidery and velvet,' so that the poet of 'Astrophel and Stella' remained for him but a 'brilliant amorist.' In that gallant and formal carriage, expressive of an age when with the grand manner went grand manners, Henley could see little more than a strut; and so he could make no acquaintance with one of the truest of the English love poets. But, when he does understand, he nearly always does it with great thoroughness; and in his best work he never fails to test even his warmest sympathy with a writer's temper by a clear apprehension of principles governing the creative energy.

On the whole, Henley stands for a quite definite thing in modern English letters. He was not a great imaginative writer, and, though he had a good style, it was not a notably distinguished one, such as, shall we say, that of Mr. Edmund Gosse. Nor, on the other hand, was he a great and original moralist, moving in lonely ways of speculation. But he did perhaps as much as any writer of his time to enlighten the ever-vexed problem of the relation of morality to art. Nothing more justly provokes suspicion in the critical mind than the art which seems to include in its purpose what the Americans call 'moral uplift.' The first sign of the critical mind, indeed, is a very proper pride in the conviction that, for better or worse, it would like to solve its own spiritual problems for itself. Such minds go to art because in that atmosphere, more perhaps than in any other, they are braced precisely for these solutions; and they rightly resent any presumption on the part of the artist that he is being sought, not for this purpose, but as a sort of spiritual ready reckoner. The critical mind is, therefore, and properly, never so touchy as when it suspects that it is being got at by the artist; and, indeed, it is a perfectly sound æsthetic instinct, since, when the artist is thinking about instructing the world instead of understanding it, he is inevitably up Queer Street.

But to understand this is by no means the same thing as to suppose that the artist ought not to concern himself with moral issues, or that he is transgressing if he plainly shows himself to be impressed by — to call it by its simplest name — goodness; and the critical mind is continually getting itself confused about this issue. It is one thing for an artist to say, 'Be good, sweet maid,' and quite another thing for him to create a Cordelia, and make it perfectly clear to us that he thinks Cordelia admirable. Every acute critic sees the defect in 'Be good, sweet maid,' but a great many critics who should know better become defensive (or offensive, as the case may be) about the Cordelias of art.

Now, Henley, as has been said already, was a good man, and he loved goodness. He was under no illusions as to what goodness really was, and, as was shown by his acrimonious treatment of some of Stevenson's whitewashers, he neither hoped nor

wanted to find paragons of virtue among men. He
was perfectly aware, too, that in this world of ex-
pediency the values of vice and virtue are continually falsified; so that he knew, for example, that
in the sum Burns was a much better man than any
of his detractors. But, when all is said, the fact
remains that Henley did immensely cherish the
ordinary decent things of charity and tolerance
and fortitude and devotion. And, while he was the
last man in the world to tell his fellows that they
ought to foster these things, he was eager in his
praises whenever he found them. Had he been a
great creative artist, his world would have been
alive with this best kind of virtue, and it would
have been his to survive the common charge of
sentimentalizing life. As he was not a great creative artist, this instinct in him found its fullest expression in criticism; and it does so in such a way
as perhaps might persuade even the most intellectual critic that, in an artist, to be moral is not
necessarily to be damned.

ALICE MEYNELL [1]

I

WHEN Alice Meynell died in 1922, she was said, I
believe, to be over seventy years of age. Anybody
less like seventy it would be difficult to imagine.
I had been honoured with her acquaintance — I
think I might almost say friendship, certainly her
good-will — for some twelve years. It was not
easy, perhaps, to think of Alice Meynell as a girl
or a young woman, but it was impossible to associate her with anything of old age. Witty, generous, of the simplest and most tender humanity,
there was also in her some austerity, not of personality, but of spirit, that suggested the women of
Greek tragedy. I have never known anyone so
ageless. Youth, maturity and fullness of years were
here strangely at one. It was in no chance moment of vision that she wrote, when she was a little
over twenty, 'A Letter from a Girl to her own Old
Age.' At twenty she was as old as she would ever
be; at her death nothing of young freshness or
wonder had gone from her. In her home, humorously intent upon the succession of family cares and
gossip, she was yet the seer always. To be with her
was to be at ease in the presence of a great lady.

[1] Read to the Royal Society of Literature from the Chair of Poetry.

Let the talk be of what it might, she was never withdrawn or indifferent; but behind the gayest of her occasions there was a quietness of mood that gave precision and authority to everything she said. Here was a perfect example of the original as distinguished from the eccentric mind. She never startled you, but she never failed to delight your attention.

II

THE custom, at present in disfavour, of printing in a poet's books good opinions of his work has been much abused. But, observed with decency, it has its uses. We may want no judgment between our own and the poetry, but we may as well not be too nice about it. It depends upon whose judgment it is. We may not need Shelley to tell us that Keats was a good poet, but we are glad that Shelley does tell us that all the same. Alice Meynell will never be with Herrick and Burns and Tennyson for everybody's reading. Her subtlety and the rareness of her manner will rather set her in public estimation with Donne and Marvell and the best of Landor. Her artistic aims were such that popular assessment is of little moment, but because of this the views of the elect among her contemporaries take on an added interest, so that there is nothing unbecoming in the page at the end of her poems that tells us what Rossetti and Francis Thompson and Coventry Patmore and Meredith had to say about her. And these and other commanding voices are emphatic in agreement that here was not merely a woman writer of talent to be courteously received, but a poet of the very finest essence. Rossetti knew her sonnet, 'Renouncement,' by heart, repeating it with high praise to the chosen; Ruskin found in her first book the finest things he had seen in modern verse; Francis Thompson foresaw the certain gathering of the best judgment of coming times in homage to her genius; Coventry Patmore, unqualified in admiration for her prose, found himself, by rather fine-spun argument, confined to saying that she was as near being a poet among the immortals as any woman could hope to be. Patmore was a poet whose best work will take a far higher place yet than it has done, but I fancy that his House of the Angels was just a touch Persian in character, and nothing is so upsetting to the intellectual Shahs of this world as the Alice Meynells. George Meredith, bringing to her a devotion from genius to genius, exquisitely revealed in the newly published volume of his letters, said of her verse, 'It has the swallow's wing, and challenges none,' and again, 'of your little collection [the first privately printed issue of a selection from the "Later Poems" of 1896] all passes into my blood, except "Parentage."' We need not go further. By right of one slender book she was admitted, when she was no older than Keats at his death, to equal fellowship with the masters of her age.

III

THIS first volume was 'Preludes,' by A. C. Thompson, published by Henry S. King and Co. in 1875, with illustrations by the poet's sister, Elizabeth Thompson, afterwards Lady Butler, the painter of 'The Roll Call.' The book contained thirty-seven poems, and it showed the poet already in the full maturity of her powers. It is, indeed, difficult to think of any English poet who in early youth has published a book in which the fulfilment of design is so complete. Other poets in their first efforts may have had a more universal, perhaps a more passionate aim, but none has subdued his intention, whatever it might be, to a more perfect mastery. The workmanship of the book is exact and unfailing from the first page to the last, and although in the poems that were to come later there was no falling away from the exquisite standard set in the beginning, there could be no development of an art that seemed to have had no probation days. It was with Alice Meynell's poetry as with her personality — first and last were one, so that we might recall the seventeenth-century epitaph:

> 'Lo, huddled here together lie
> Green youth, grey age, white infancy.'

'Preludes' at once displays the characteristics that have become familiar to the poet's admirers. Its general mood is one of affectionate resignation, with neither bitterness nor even regret. Throughout there is a spiritual humility that reminds us how little of true pride there is in the common self-assertions. There is here a surrender of soul, but it is consciously a surrender of something so rare and lovely that it can be made only to a supremely imagined purity. The poet is humble only because of the divine company in which she moves. This accounts for the fact that one note for which we commonly look in the poetry of youth, that of revolt, is entirely absent from 'Preludes.' Anger and protest and denunciation, those ardours of rebellion that stir most generous young minds as they first realize the tyrannies of a stupid world, were nothing to this poet, who, however she might look upon the vulgar errors of society, could not conceive of them as food for the imagination. Not that she was careless of these errors on the one hand, or that her poetry was mere placidity on the other — nothing could be wider of the mark than to suppose either of these things. She took always a very practical, and even argumentative, interest in the thousand ways in which man teases and confounds himself in the ordering of his communities, but these were matters for the tea-table, not for the seclusions of art. Such conflicts as these implied were, indeed, crude and journalistic beside those finer and more decisive conflicts that were moving always in her poetry. Scolding is well enough, necessary at least, but you may scold here to-day and there to-morrow, and it's pretty much all one; but to possess your soul is a much more intricate and ponderable business, and there must be no wasted strokes since the stake now to be won is for a lifetime, or eternity perhaps. Insensitive ears deafened by the tumult of nations catch nothing of such campaigns as went forward in Alice Meynell's poetry, but it is none the less by such as these that the liberation of man must come.

Looking within this general mood, we may detect certain qualities of mind that were peculiarly Alice Meynell's own. First, perhaps, of these is an amazing gift for capturing with a phrase the most elusive turns of thought, for arresting the cloud shadows of emotions as they pass over the mind and giving them solid intellectual form. This was a faculty that she shared with her beloved seventeenth-century lyrists, with Donne and Crashaw and Vaughan, but in actual deftness of its exercise I think she excelled them all. Such poets as those, perhaps, burnt more fiercely than she, and were even more curious in spiritual skill, but none of them gave difficult thought so lucid a simplicity of statement. It is this that we find in

THE YOUNG NEOPHYTE

Who knows what days I answer for to-day?
    Giving the bud I give the flower. I bow
    This yet unfaded and a faded brow;
Bending these knees and feeble knees, I pray.

Thoughts yet unripe in me I bend one way,
    Give one repose to pain I know not now,
    One check to joy that comes, I guess not how.
I dedicate my fields when Spring is grey.

O rash! (I smile) to pledge my hidden wheat.
    I fold to-day at altars far apart
Hands trembling with what toils? In their retreat

    I seal my love to-be, my folded art.
I light the tapers at my head and feet,
    And lay the crucifix on this silent heart.

And even more remarkably in

THE VISITING SEA

As the inhastening tide doth roll,
Home from the deep, along the whole
    Wide shining strand, and floods the caves,
      — Your love came filling with happy waves
The open sea-shore of my soul.

But inland from the seaward spaces,
None knows, not even you, the places
    Brimmed, at your coming, out of sight,
      — The little solitudes of delight
This tide constrains in dim embraces.

You see the happy shore, wave-rimmed,
But know not of the quiet dimmed

> Rivers your coming floods and fills,
> The little pools 'mid happier hills,
> My silent rivulets, over-brimmed.
>
> What, I have secrets from you? Yes.
> But, visiting Sea, your love doth press
> And reach in further than you know,
> And fills all these; and, when you go,
> There's loneliness in loneliness.

And, as a final example, the reader should turn to the longer 'Letter from a Girl to her own Old Age.'

Together with this power of saying exactly what we might have supposed could not have been said even nebulously, a power constant in Alice Meynell's poetry, is the less rare but not less admirable power of sending tides of imaginative suggestion through a plain statement, and employed by this poet with most beautiful assurance, nowhere more strikingly than in 'Parted,' and particularly in the last stanza:

> 'He is not banished, for the showers
> Yet wake this green warm earth of ours.
> How can the summer but be sweet?
> I shall not have him at my feet,
> And yet my feet are on the flowers.'

The intellectual ingenuity of which I have been speaking is, more than most material, under the necessity of proving itself in poetry, of coming into complete artistic life. More commonplace content matter — the mere declaration of love, let us say, or the telling of the seasons, or the thought of death's certainty — may fail, because of insufficient emotional pressure, to quicken into poetry, but although the failure may be complete, we can pass by without resentment. But there are pretensions in subtle and remote metaphysical inquiry that cannot escape so easily if they do not justify themselves in poetry. The failure in such a case becomes openly ridiculous, and even offensive. The conceits of seventeenth-century poetry, lovely when they were fortunate, as they so often were, could easily enough become merely silly, or, at their worst, revolting. The love lyric could become a deliberate exercise in insincerity, and the religious lyric could sometimes smell like a slaughter-house. Alice Meynell's poetry is in this matter as unfailingly certain as in everything else that it undertook. The conception may be as intellectually arbitrary as the devices of the schoolmen, but it flowers always in her verse into pure and inevitable truth. What, in its abstraction, could be more fantastic than this, 'To the Beloved,' for example, and yet what could be more tenderly convincing?

To The Beloved

Oh, not more subtly silence strays
   Amongst the winds, between the voices,
Mingling alike with pensive lays,
   And with the music that rejoices,
Than thou art present in my days.

My silence, life returns to thee
In all the pauses of her breath.
Hush back to rest the melody
That out of thee awakeneth;
And thou, wake ever, wake for me!

Thou art like silence all unvexed,
Though wild words part my soul from thee.
Thou art like silence unperplexed,
A secret and a mystery
Between one footfall and the next.

Most dear pause in a mellow lay!
Thou art inwoven with every air.
With thee the wildest tempests play,
And snatches of thee everywhere
Make little heavens throughout the day.

Darkness and solitude shine, for me.
For life's fair outward part are rife
The silver noises; let them be.
It is the very soul of life
Listens for thee, listens for thee.

O pause between the sobs of cares;
O thought within all thought that is;
Trance between laughters unawares:
Thou art the shape of melodies,
And thou the ecstasy of prayers!

Alice Meynell, writing but little, never wrote
insignificantly, and each of her few poems presents
its own attractive problems; but already in her first
book certain themes are recurrent, and certain distinctions of style assert themselves. The communion of a mind with its other self, sometimes

moving in its own recesses, sometimes in the person of a friend or lover, is one of her favourite pre-occupations. It is to be found in 'The Young Neophyte,' 'The Visiting Sea,' and the 'Girl's Letter,' and more than once elsewhere, as in

THE SPRING TO THE SUMMER

The Poet sings to her Poet

O Poet of the time to be,
My conqueror, I began for thee.
    Enter into thy poet's pain,
    And take the riches of the rain,
And make the perfect year for me.

Thou unto whom my lyre shall fall,
Whene'er thou comest, hear my call.
    Oh, keep the promise of my lays,
    Take thou the parable of my days;
I trust thee with the aim of all.

And if thy thoughts unfold from me,
Know that I too have hints of thee,
    Dim hopes that come across my mind
    In the rare days of warmer wind,
And tones of summer in the sea.

And I have set thy paths, I guide
Thy blossoms on the wild hillside.
    And I, thy bygone poet, share
    The flowers that throng thy feet where'er
I led thy feet before I died.

This sense of an intimacy, a mystical understanding, that makes many things — perhaps, in the philosophic conclusion of the matter, all things —

one, is, together with the instinct for surrender in
service to some divine wisdom that alone can command service from a spirit so rare, the prevailing
mood communicated by 'Preludes,' and indeed by
the later poems as well. 'A poet of one mood in all
my lays,' she says, of herself we must suppose, and
shapes of the world are subjected, in all their
variety, to the influence of this mood, which is
rightly the way of poetry.

> 'The countries change, but not the west-wind days
>   Which are my songs.'

It is only the trivial mind that will confuse this
constancy of character with monotony. What is
said does not lose its charm or pungency, or even
its surprise, because we can recognize always the
tones of the voice. The waters of 'Preludes' flow,
it is true, narrowly between rather high banks, but
they are deep and fresh always. The poet was
keeping the time, she tells us, sacred

> 'To all the miles and miles of unsprung wheat,
> And to the Spring waiting beyond the portal,
> And to the future of my own young art.'

But the future was more than suggested in the
present. The mood was grown, the art practised
and sure. Already the manner had that curious
fastidiousness that was to mark it always, and to
mark it apart. It was a manner rarely compounded,
reticent, and yet precise and uncompromising in
statement, shunning every kind of emphasis, and

yet of the most lucid and ringing accent, shy of rich colours in diction, and yet making hard and prosaic phrases flush and glow with unexpected light.

The Lover Urges the Better Thrift

My Fair, no beauty of thine will last
    Save in my love's eternity.
    Thy smiles, that light thee fitfully,
Are lost for ever — their moment past —
    Except the few thou givest to me.

Thy sweet words vanish day by day,
    As all breath of mortality;
    Thy laughter, done, must cease to be,
And all thy dear tones pass away,
    Except the few that sing to me.

Hide them within my heart, oh, hide
    All thou art loth should go from thee.
    Be kinder to thyself and me.
My cupful from this river's tide
    Shall never reach the long sad sea.

Lyric poetry could hardly be simpler than that, and at the same time it could hardly be subtler, or even more complex. It is an art of which we may well speak, as she of her own 'Daisy' —

    'Thou little veil for so great mystery.'

It never fails; it can hardly be said ever to falter even. Just once, in

    'Was earth cold or sunny, Sweet,
      At the coming of your feet?'

there is a moment of uneasiness, but it passes, and

is alone in the book. For a young poet so proudly of tradition, and so spiritually akin to one age at least of English verse, there is a surprising absence of apparent influences upon the actual phrasing of the poems. In the line about flowers —

'When they blossom from thy dust —'

there is a direct reminiscence of Shirley, but I do not think 'Preludes' has another echo of the kind.

IV

'Poems' appeared in 1896, twenty-one years after 'Preludes,' but it was only a reprint of the earlier book with the addition of seven new poems, among them 'Renouncement,' the sonnet of Rossetti's admiration, and the 'Song of Derivations,' to which further reference will be made. In the same year appeared a small privately printed pamphlet, 'Other Poems,' containing ten pieces that in turn formed more than half the slender 'Later Poems' of 1902. Then followed another silence, this time of fifteen years, to be broken in 1917 by 'A Father of Women and Other Poems,' in which the poet added no more than sixteen short poems to her collected work, now amounting to some eighty poems, covering a working period of over forty years. Finally, in 'Last Poems,' published posthumously, there is the last and relatively large addition of another thirty-one poems, and the whole work is now available in a single definitive volume. In this volume, small in size as the product of a long life, made up almost entirely of short lyrics, and yet very close and exacting in substance, there is hardly a stanza or even a line that the severest critical judgment would wish away. And yet of the work after 1875 there is little that is essential to be said that might not as well have been suggested by the first volume. The delight never fails, but it is not the less eagerly welcomed because it is not a new delight. It is the measure of Alice Meynell's excellence as a poet that after we know a dozen of her poems we feel that there is no possible further chance of novelty from her, and yet that there will never be a failure of complete and arresting originality. The more familiar we become with her work the more do we want it to go on being just what it is without change. In the later books the poetic life of 'Preludes' is modified here and emphasized there, but no more, and we would not have it otherwise. On the whole there is, perhaps, a little more to question — that is to say, we are pulled up once in fifty pages now instead of once in seventy as before. Every now and again, very rarely, we wonder whether the intellectual deftness and the balanced mastery of language are not playing half a trick with the poet. One of her most celebrated lyrics is the

CRADLE-SONG AT TWILIGHT

The child not yet is lulled to rest.
  Too young a nurse, the slender Night
So laxly holds him to her breast
  That throbs with flight.

He plays with her, and will not sleep.
  For other playfellows she sighs;
An unmaternal fondness keep
  Her alien eyes.

It is idle to praise a thing so exquisitely done; the mastery is plain at once. And yet is there in its nature something not false but capricious, capricious in the presence of truth? Has the delight in saying a thing so beautifully for once led the poet from imagination to make-believe? Does the night do any of these things — how is she too young a nurse? One sees the fancy, but is it more than that — is there in the lyric the inescapable argument that is at the roots of all fine poetry, at the roots nearly always of Alice Meynell's? Again, this from 'The Rainy Summer':

'No scents may pause within the garden-fold;
  The rifled flowers are cold as ocean-shells;
Bees, humming in the storm, carry their cold
  Wild honey to cold cells.'

How perfectly done — what aristocracy of writing — but are the cells cold? I'm not sure, but I somehow do not think they are, and poetry in this sense should not be feigning.[1] The same occasional

[1] The case is different when the poet is genuinely mistaken as to his facts.

tendency shows itself in one or two other poems, where the thought, instead of being subtle and suggestive as it is in most of this poet's work, becomes odd, wilful.

WHY WILT THOU CHIDE?

Why wilt thou chide,
Who hast attained to be denied?
    Oh learn, above
All price is my refusal, Love.
    My sacred Nay
Was never cheapened by the way.
Thy single sorrow crowns thee lord
Of an unpurchasable word.

O strong, O pure!
As Yea makes happier loves secure
    I vow thee this
Unique rejection of a kiss.
    I guard for thee
This jealous sad monopoly.
I seal this honour thine; none dare
Hope for a part in thy despair.

I, for one, who adore Alice Meynell's work and think of it as among the very fine flowers of the English genius, do not much care for the poet who wrote that poem — I somehow do not think that in strict terms of the imagination she really meant it. Meredith, in liking the first instalment of the later poem, made a reservation, as I mentioned, in the case of 'Parentage.' This is the poem:

'Ah, no, not these!
These, who were childless, are not they who gave

So many dead unto the journeying wave,
The helpless nurselings of the cradling seas;
Not they who doomed by infallible decrees
Unnumbered man to the innumerable grave.

'But those who slay
Are fathers. Theirs are armies. Death is theirs;
The death of innocences and despairs;
The dying of the golden and the grey.
The sentence, when these speak it, has no Nay.
And she who slays is she who bears, who bears.'

Writing of this to the poet, Meredith says: 'Appealing to our common mother for an explanation of her favoured daughter's mood when writing it, I had this from my Fount of Wisdom: "She has the gift of splitting a hair into a million threads, and seeing the various hues in shade, and she can still be tempted to play upon her faculty, and on a wet afternoon she may consent to a musical diversion in pessimistic pathos. It is not the 'soul of her soul.'" So speaks Nature to me.'

We may leave it at that, and with it all questioning whatsoever.

Among the later poems are a few pieces that are more definitely occasional in character than anything in the first book, 'November Blue,' 'A Dead Harvest,' and 'The Watershed,' for example, but they are all beautifully done, and earn their place truly enough. Here and there is a touch of more explicit humour than we had found before, as in

THE LADY POVERTY

The Lady Poverty was fair:
But she has lost her looks of late,
With change of times and change of air.
Ah slattern! she neglects her hair,
Her gown, her shoes; she keeps no state
As once when her pure feet were bare.

Or — almost worse, if worse can be —
She scolds in parlours, dusts and trims,
Watches and counts.   Oh, is this she
Whom Francis met, whose step was free,
Who with Obedience carolled hymns,
In Umbria walked with Chastity?

Where is her ladyhood? Not here,
Not among modern kinds of men;
But in the stony fields, where clear
Through the thin trees the skies appear,
In delicate spare soil and fen,
And slender landscape and austere.

We find sometimes, too, a more objective mood
asserting itself, directed now upon problems of
literary criticism, producing the specialized kind of
poetry that William Watson has done so well, and
in which Alice Meynell is certainly his equal, and
again upon problems and aspects of modern civilization, as in the lovely and rather unexpected
'Threshing Machine.' But for the most part the
poetry of the later years is with that of the earlier,
both in its concerns and in its methods. We have
the same slow gracious movement of the verse, the

same limpidity of phrase, the same fixed and piercing vision.

THE SHEPHERDESS

She walks — the lady of my delight —
    A shepherdess of sheep.
Her flocks are thoughts. She keeps them white:
    She guards them from the steep;
She feeds them on the fragrant height,
    And folds them in for sleep.

She roams maternal hills and bright,
    Dark valleys safe and deep.
Into that tender breast at night
    The chastest stars may peep.
She walks — the lady of my delight ·
    A shepherdess of sheep.

She holds her little thoughts in sight,
    Though gay they run and leap.
She is so circumspect and right;
    She has her soul to keep.
She walks — the lady of my delight —
    A shepherdess of sheep.

The line 'She is so circumspect and right' might almost stand in a phrase as the key to Alice Meynell's style. It is the style always of a poet who possessed her soul and her imagination, one who was in the great line of English lyrists, and yet stamping personality upon every word she wrote. As we read her work we realize that the independence is complete, and yet the loyalty that exalts it is splendid. Original genius never paid more perfect tribute to its ancestry than here in

A Song of Derivations

I come from nothing; but from where
Come the undying thoughts I bear?
　Down, through long links of death and birth,
　From the past poets of the earth.
My immortality is there.

I am like the blossom of an hour.
But long, long vanished sun and shower
　Awoke my breath i' the young world's air.
　I track the past back everywhere
Through seed and flower and seed and flower.

Or I am like a stream that flows
Full of the cold springs that arose
　In morning lands, in distant hills;
　And down the plain my channel fills
With melting of forgotten snows.

Voices, I have not heard, possessed
My own fresh songs; my thoughts are blessed
　With relics of the far unknown.
　And mixed with memories not my own
The sweet streams throng into my breast.

Before this life began to be,
The happy songs that wake in me
　Woke long ago and far apart.
　Heavily on this little heart
Presses this immortality.

A. E. HOUSMAN'S 'LAST POEMS'

'Now dreary dawns the eastern light,
    And fall of eve is drear,
And cold the poor man lies at night,
    And so goes out the year.

'Little is the luck I've had,
    And oh, 'tis comfort small
To think that many another lad
    Has had no luck at all.'

THAT clearly is the expression of a tragic mood,
almost even a forlorn one which is less than tragic.
And the note pervades Mr. Housman's new book.
Even such occasional relief as is found in his longest
poem 'Hell-Gate,' with its final overthrow of the
black city, or in

'O Queen of air and darkness,
    I think 'tis truth you say,
And I shall die to-morrow;
    But you will die to-day,'

hardly modifies the extremely grim character of
this beautiful collection of poems. The passionate,
brooding protest, that came out of the west-mid-
land landscape twenty-five years ago, is unchanged.
To say that the technique of 'Last Poems' is better
than that of the best of the 'Shropshire Lad' would
be to say that the impossible had been achieved.

But it is as good, and more consistently good. The little poem at the head of this paper is perfectly done, and hardly a page of the book fails to match it. The old manner is often here, but it is no less arresting because Mr. Housman himself happens to have done it before.

> 'When summer's end is nighing,
>   And skies at evening cloud,
> I muse on change and fortune
>   And all the feats I vowed
>   When I was young and proud. . . .'

So, it would seem, in these poems where the loved landscape is now rather one of recollection, the youth that once saw so much bitterness in the promise of life has passed to a maturity when the old fears have but proved themselves. Circumstance itself, as apart from a general philosophic view of life, would seem to have worked to the same end.

> 'When I would muse in boyhood
>   The wild green woods among,
> And nurse resolves and fancies
>   Because the world was young,
> It was not foes to conquer,
>   Nor sweethearts to be kind,
> But it was friends to die for
>   That I would seek and find.
>
> 'I sought them far and found them,
>   The sure, the straight, the brave,
> The hearts I lost my own to,
>   The souls I could not save.
> They braced their belts about them,

They crossed in ships the sea,
They sought and found six feet of ground,
And there they died for me.'

And yet the consoling thing about this book is that it vindicates anew the belief that art, truly done, however desolate its mood, can never be desolating in its effect. It is not merely the fact that the poet here faces his tragic conclusions with so fine a courage that makes the book, when all is said, an inspiring one. The truth is that despair is no longer despair when it ceases to be dumb. Perfect expression, such as it finds over and over again in Mr. Housman's new poems, purges despair of its own disastrousness and transfigures it into a mood that knows not only to endure, but even to delight. If one had to say in other words what Mr. Housman thinks of the world, it would be no very inspiriting story. But as we listen to his statement, made in terms of an exquisite poetic art, we know that there is a beauty which is not at the mercy of any philosophic denial.

EDWIN ARLINGTON ROBINSON [1]

WHEN recently Mr. Edwin Arlington Robinson reached his fiftieth birthday, he was publicly greeted by nearly every poet of any distinction in America as the master of them all. Enlightened criticism in that country has for long recognized him as having more clearly the qualities of permanence, perhaps, than any other American now writing. Even a poet so unlike Mr. Robinson himself in aim and method as Miss Amy Lowell devotes a long chapter in her book on 'Tendencies in American Poetry' to the work of one whose distinction she finely acknowledges. A new book by Mr. Robinson has in America, among the austere critics at least, as much importance, shall we say, as a new book by Mr. Yeats has to those in this country. And yet, with all this, there is, I suppose, no poet of anything like his excellence in America who is there so little known as more than a name, while in this country at present he can hardly be said even to be a name. [2] In reviewing a recently issued anthology of contemporary American verse, at the length of two columns, the 'Times Literary Supplement'

[1] Read to the Royal Society of Literature from the Chair of Poetry.
[2] I leave these words as they were written, though happily they could be modified to-day.

passed him by without reference, while the 'Nation and Athenæum,' with even less excuse, since in that case it could not be merely an oversight, spoke of him only to dismiss him in two or three lines as being duller than Wordsworth at his dullest. A third writer, in the 'Saturday Review,' can only say that his 'compositions are to a strange degree' like those of Miss Amy Lowell and Mr. Sandburg. It would be as intelligent to say that the poems of Edgar Allan Poe are like those of Walt Whitman. Ignorance is all very well, and even rather charming in its place, but when it begins to commit absurdities of this kind something ought to be done about it. A critic who discusses contemporary American poetry and thinks that Mr. Robinson is either not worth mentioning at all or only to be mentioned with contempt, or that his poetry is like Mr. Sandburg's, simply does not know his business and ought to change it for another. He might, for example, just as well treat Mr. Robert Bridges so, in talking of contemporary English poetry. American literature to-day is far fuller of interest than many people in this country think. Most of our young novelists would willingly allow at least half a dozen of their fellows in America to be among the most important contributors to their art in this generation, and every poet here who knows anything about it would say as much on his side. Take them or leave them, you cannot dismiss as insignificant such poets as Amy Lowell, Edgar Lee Masters, Vachel Lindsay, Robert Frost, Carl Sandburg, and, as it seems to me, more decisively even than these, Edwin Arlington Robinson. Again, in literary criticism the Americans are doing a great deal of notable work. It is true that they are also doing much that does not seem to matter, being, as it were, a restatement in a local idiom of what are now commonplaces of older cultures. The country is rich in critics who escape being dull without the sacrifice of erudition. At the same time it is in criticism, perhaps, more than in any other form of literary activity, that some peculiarly American defects most clearly show themselves. No modern writing more commonly indulges the fallacy that the only escape from academic tameness is to be found in a smart impertinence which is fondly supposed to be intellectual candour. A critic like Mr. Heywood Broun can always distinguish between being entertaining and being tiresomely bright, but some of his fellows can make wit an incomparable tedium. It is such as these that have from time to time spoken of Mr. Robinson much in the manner of the 'Nation' reviewer here. But while we writers have much to learn from the best of our American friends in matters of freshness and enterprise, this particular kind of example is one that should rather warn than instruct us.

Mr. Robinson has throughout his career taken as little pains to attract public attention to himself in any way, except by the excellence of his work, as, say, has Thomas Hardy. He has never been a figure for the paragraphists, and he has shown that it is possible for one of the most distinguished men of his time to hide himself very successfully in the glare of New York. His life and manner have just that incisive reticence that is so characteristic of his poetry. For some years this most sensitive poet was in his fortunes, as they say, down and out. One feels that it would hardly have occurred to him to take any steps to mend matters, and it is an amusing and not uninstructive comment upon American life that it was Theodore Roosevelt who found him and insisted on giving him an official post, seeing to it that the authorities should recognize that Robinson's first business was poetry. There was a gallantry in this, and one is glad of it, but it meant less to Mr. Robinson, one is sure, than it would even to most poets in the same circumstances. His tender, ironical, fearless genius has in it a peculiar stability that would surely make him less dependent on surroundings than are more mercurial creators. To direct a tranquillity of contemplation upon the whirlpools of life is in a rare degree the function of his art, and, for all his vivid reaction to that life, even at its most violent, we feel that the tranquillity is one that nothing could shake. Mr. Robinson was acclaimed as leader by the American poets of his time, but of the qualities which differentiate most of their work as a group from poetry in general there is scarcely a trace to be found in Robinson's verse. A poet has a perfect right to his own choice of material, and nothing is so critically inept as to blame him for it, whatever it may be. The only question is whether he has transfigured it into the reality of art. It may be that the material does not interest us, but that is our own affair and not the poet's, and when we say that it does not interest us it generally means that we are less interested in poetry than in our own preoccupations and points of view. It is the merest futility to argue with a poet about his conclusions, and it is only worth while to analyze the content matter of his work when we happen to find that this work does, because of its poetic virtue, move us profoundly. It is then, and not till then, that the material of his art is of any concern to us. It is just as with our affections for people. Out of his love the lover finds an ever-quickening interest in all that the beloved is, in points of character and processes of the mind. But it is love that begets this interest, and not the interest which begets love; love being, as it were, the life of human contact, as the poetic essence is to the whole body of a poet's work. So in poetry we may care very much for a poet whose philosophic and moral temper is not at all in general sympathy with our own, and, on the other hand, we may find no profit in another who flatters us exactly in these things. For example, there is a great deal in the material of Shelley's poetry which, for its own sake, means little or nothing to me, and yet his poetry stirs me as much, perhaps, as any in the world; while on strictly reasonable grounds I should agree with almost everything that Miss Willcox says in her verse, and yet it does not begin to stir me at all. Consequently, I am really interested in the content matter of Shelley's poetry even when I do not agree with his point of view, while I am not at all interested in that of Miss Willcox even when I do. I see the virtue in the content matter of such poets as Mr. Sandburg, because in some measure I am moved by their art to begin with, but it is no disparagement to them to say that Mr. Robinson's content matter seems to be more important, which simply means that Mr. Robinson's art does, for me at least, make a more certain appeal.

The difference, then, between Mr. Robinson's preoccupation and that of nearly all the so-called modern school who have acclaimed him, is that for them all the clamorous accidents of our civilization have become an absorbing and sometimes a tragic experience in themselves, as though the very noise had startled them into a conviction that it was in itself a fundamental and significant thing. The roar and the savagery and the reek which are a part of Chicago, for example, seem to provoke Mr. Sandburg into a kind of determination to answer them back in their own terms, and he does it with courage and mastery. This does not mean that he has not other perceptions as well, but this perception does loom very largely in his poetic mood. And so it is with poets like Mr. Vachel Lindsay and, in a more rustic manner, Mr. Lee Masters and Mr. Frost, and, allowing for all her varied and traditional scholarship, Miss Amy Lowell. But for Mr. Robinson these things hardly exist at all. When they do he only turns to them as an occasional poet, momentarily disturbed from his habitual concerns as he might be by a street accident. His preoccupation is the spirit of man, not assailed and tortured by that movement of life which we call civilization, but seen, as it were, detached from this influence and labouring in all the ironies and aspirations of its own nature. Mr. Robinson is in the true Greek tradition in this, that whereas most of his fellow-countrymen who are poets see man beset by society, which is circumstance, he sees man beset by his own character, which is fate.

Again, unlike most of his American contemporaries, Mr. Robinson in his verse structure is almost always traditional. With hardly an exception throughout his collected poems he uses the normal blank verse line, the four- or six- or eight-lined rhymed stanza, generally with four or five beats to the line, and masters these with his own rhythmic personality, as practically every great poet in the English language has done these five hundred years. At the risk of repeating what I have said before elsewhere, the commonest error of a certain school of critics and poets is that they continually confuse the functions and virtues of metre with those of rhythm. Metrical forms are slowly evolved in the cumulative consciousness of a race, and their acceptance by a succession of poets is governed by their peculiar fitness to the genius of the language. No individual mind at this time of day, for example, could possibly discover beyond all argument that, whereas the five-foot iambic line is a perfect vehicle for the expression in English of a very wide range of poetic feeling, the Alexandrine is, broadly speaking, of no use at all for the English language. That is to say, we could drop the Alexandrine from our poetry entirely without any likely loss at all, whereas the exclusion of our normal blank verse line would be an extremely heavy loss to every future poet. But we are to-day aware of this, not through sudden revelation to our own understanding, but because of an instinct bred out of five centuries of poetic practice. And the poet who thinks that by submitting himself, not slavishly but as a true inheritor, to this condition of his art he is in some way stunting his own personality, confuses self-respect with egomania, and is fit not for Parnassus but for Bedlam. The lucid poet knows that within those metrical forms there is infinite scope for the impress of his own rhythmic sense, and he knows that in this collaboration between tradition and his invention is the only sure hope of any poetic completeness. Mr. Robinson is with the masters of his art in recognizing this without question, almost, it would seem, without conscious choice. And of his metrical manner no more need be said than that.

The rhythmic life itself within his verse is very subtly governed by his whole poetic character. In reading poetry one becomes more and more aware of a curious distinction between two groups, in one or the other of which almost every poet can be placed. It is clearly a mistake to suggest that great poetry can be turned into prose without destruction of its meaning, but it is true that some great poets, even in their most impassioned work, have what may be called a prose quality, while others have not. There are two kinds of magic in poetry, that of precision and that of suggestion, and preference for one above the other may remain a matter of individual taste. In the first group I should place such poets as Milton, Matthew Arnold, Wordsworth and Mr. Robinson, while in the second such as Coleridge, the Keats of 'La Belle Dame,' Edgar Allan Poe, and Mr. de la Mare.

And for some of us that quality of precision results in a still lucidity which is more poignant and magical than any glamorous world of whispers and shadows. However this may be, Mr. Robinson's poetry is from beginning to end informed always by this quality in a very marked degree, and it is a quality that gives his rhythm its unmistakable character. His music is never languorous, or slow, or trembling, or remote. It is, rather, always perfectly clear in its modulation, simple in its accent, and yet as full always of delightful surprise as that of any of the most delicate weavers of suggestion. His is rather a tragic world, generally a deeply tragic world. He celebrates it not in the haunted cadences of sorceresses round the fire but with the clear melodic ease of a well-voiced countryman at the inn. 'Flammonde' is an admirable example of Mr. Robinson's manner, and it is very suggestive both as to the quality and the interests of his mind. Over and over again in this poem are instances of that exquisite clarity of which I have been speaking:

> 'What small satanic sort of kink
>   Was in his brain? What broken link
>   Withheld him from the destinies
>   That came so near to being his?'

and again,

> 'Nor need we now, since he knew best,
>   Nourish an ethical unrest. . . .'

Such things as these seem to me to be consummate in their mastery, touching the farthest difficulties of poetic writing. The modern English poet who does the same kind of thing most surely is, I think, Mrs. Meynell. She, too, knows the virtue of such exact, uncompromising words. It is when a poet writes with this measured certainty, rather than with the vehemence of frustration, that we know that emotion is moving most deeply. The false critics of poetry are constantly confusing this steady incandescence with the cold and passionless, looking rather for crude colours and protestations and wistful stammerings as the signs of poetry. But the wise reader knows that directly he comes to this kind of chastity in writing, when the virtues of the finest prose are informed with the magic of poetry, he is in the regions of the rarest poetic discovery. Suddenly to find such lines as these just quoted and repeated is to be at the heart of beauty and pathos, and Mr. Robinson with great art constantly moves from such lines to a yet barer simplicity, and with

> 'And women, young and old, were fond
> Of looking at the man Flammonde. . . .'

and

> 'We've each a darkening hill to climb;
> And this is why, from time to time
> In Tilbury Town, we look beyond
> Horizons for the man Flammonde.'

brings us very near to tears. I know, indeed, of hardly any poet in the language who more surely or constantly communicates a sense of tragic pity. There can be no greater praise, and yet I do not think it is too great, than to say that passages like those quoted, and they are common in Mr. Robinson's work, remind us of the supreme close of 'Samson Agonistes.'

> 'Nothing is here for tears, nothing to wail
> Or knock the breast, no weakness, no contempt,
> Dispraise or blame, nothing but well and fair,
> And what may quiet us in a death so noble.'

It is not within the scope of this study to make a close analysis of the whole of Mr. Robinson's work in all its many kinds. His 'Collected Poems' fill six hundred pages and range from the smallest lyric of occasion to narrative poems of three thousand lines in length. Nor, for that matter, is it ever very profitable to explain in detail what a poet is writing about, since what he says can be said only in the way that he says it. One can but point out his general methods and note the tendencies of his moods. 'Flammonde' represents very fairly a common way with Mr. Robinson. The man who is kept from 'the destinies which come so near to being his' is constantly in his thought, and there is a large group of poems in which he figures, in great psychological variety but always with the same poignancy. 'My dreams have all come true for other men,' says one of his derelict heroes, and the poet sees character bewildered and mired no less among the romantic glories of Arthur's court than in the slums of New York. With this tragic sense we find nearly always in his work an ironic touch which makes it not only moving but always interesting, or, as Rossetti had it, amusing. Since Mr. Robinson is a poet, it is needless to say that in this irony there is no touch of cynicism, though severity is not unknown to it. He can not only give character single statement, as in the Flammonde poem, but he can show it very finely in conflict, as in 'Llewellyn and the Tree,' a poem of perfect dramatic proportions with its deft conclusion:

> 'He may be near us, dreaming yet
>   Of unrepented rouge and coral;
> Or in a grave without a name
>   May be as far off as a moral.'

'As far off as a moral.' That is one of Mr. Robinson's charming touches of irony. Perhaps the silliest affectation of a rather assertive school of contemporary criticism is that poetry and moral conviction cannot live together, or that, at least, if a poet has moral convictions the only decent thing he can do is to be quiet about them. One has only to say over to one's self Shakespeare, Milton, Burns, Blake, Wordsworth, Shelley, Browning, to reduce the whole theory to nonsense, but it is nevertheless one very commonly advanced in these days. A particular critic may have no interest in a particular poet's moral substance, but that has nothing to do with the question. No poet asks the critic's suffrage in this matter, nor is it in any way his purpose to impose his own moral conviction upon anybody else. Wordsworth's moral conviction may or may not be of importance to me, but it is of immense importance to him, and that is what matters in the economy of the world. Without it his poetry simply would not have existed; it is, in fact, the very soil out of which the flowers of that poetry spring. It may be true that the soil here and there runs a little thin, but nobody reasonably looks for uniform perfection even in a great poet. The point is that the critics who accuse a poet like Wordsworth of a too prevalent desire to improve the occasion are mere virtuosi playing with the great passions of the world that Wordsworth so fully lived. It is the old story; it does not matter at all what the particular nature of the poet's moral conclusions may be. No moral worlds could be more dissimilar than those of, say, Wordsworth and Shelley and Swinburne, but in each case the poetry of these men was just a condition of his own moral world informed by genius and nothing else whatever. And every poet of importance from Æschylus down to Mr. Robinson has fearlessly recognized this principle in his art. Mr. Robinson wants to instruct no one; but moral purpose and pity burn passionately, though with a quiet flame, throughout his work, and when a critic tells us that he finds him duller than Wordsworth at his dullest we have a perfect epitome of nearly all that is false in the aforesaid school of criticism.

MR. MASEFIELD'S 'REYNARD' AND 'RIGHT ROYAL'

Upon nothing in us, perhaps, do the changes of the years mark themselves more clearly than upon our affection for poetry. In early youth we go to the poets for that glowing aura of romantic sensibility which they most commonly achieve when they themselves are young. It is then that most surely we feel the spell of Byron, of the more ethereal quality in Shelley, of such lesser masters as Poe and Thomas Moore. Shelley, it need not be said, can supply our later needs as well, and superbly, but in much of his work he is with these others as satisfying the desire of youth for that cloudier beauty where clear definition stands for little beside the mere rush of enchantment. As we come to middle age our demand is more and more for the concrete image, the hard outline, the intellectual clarity that is behind all larger vision, be it never so radiant. It is then that we realize the true lyric mastery of such men as Marvell, and Donne, and Wordsworth of the shorter poems, and Blake, and Landor. What happens in old age I cannot say, since with that Time waits upon me yet.

But there is one kind of poetry which, if we care for it at all, we care for always. In its nature it may conceivably be said that this is not of the very rarest attar, that it never quite touches the supreme wonder of phrase that is the last delight of poetry. But for all that it seems to me that it has more uniformly than any other poetic kind what we mean by greatness. It is the poetry that takes easily into its processes great vistas of humanity with their background. The highest masters, such as Shakespeare, can by habit encompass this end and at the same time touch their work at every point with the rarer precision of which I have spoken. Others in their creative impetus passing humanity under rapid review may inform their work less frequently with the high lights of distinction, and yet by the very liberality and sweep of their perceptions come to greatness. The most notable example of this kind is Chaucer, and with him William Morris may fairly claim rank.

And now in 'Reynard the Fox' and 'Right Royal' Mr. Masefield has added this distinction to many that were already his. His lyrics, at their best, have a tenderness that is not surpassed in contemporary poetry. In his previous narrative poems he has been able to bring this tenderness to longer work that has always seemed to me to be essentially lyric in character. The most affecting quality in 'The Everlasting Mercy' and 'The Daffodil Fields' and the rest of them is that same tenderness relating Mr. Masefield's own personal-.

ity to the people of whom, and the events of which, he is writing. We do not quarrel with this; we are grateful for it, as we are always when beauty is the end. But with 'Reynard the Fox' there was a change. It would not be difficult to select a passage here and there for the isolated beauty which is common in the other poems, but here it would be to miss the presiding excellence of the work. In this poem and the later 'Right Royal' a motley of life passes with a gusto that is new in Mr. Masefield's work and brings it far more nearly than it has been before into the region of Chaucer's profound and moving comedy.

It is a habit of mind with most people who think about poetry to give to the narrative a relatively humble rank in the art, and it is a habit which Mr. Masefield is constantly challenging by his work nowadays. Here is a poet, whose lyric and tragic notes are as sure as any of his time, turning repeatedly from these to the call of romantic narrative. It often happens that this peculiar method has a certain narcotic quality which, although it is invaluable in the scheme of things, does generally mean a slackening of imagination. It accounts for the difference between a great man like Dumas and a greater man like Shakespeare. Dumas, probably, has loyaller readers than any other writer in our modern literature. That is to say, people who read Dumas at all return to him over and over again.

But the return is nearly always made from a more or less tired or distracted mood. Then it is that the magnificent narrative power and the slightly unreal ethical world of Dumas combine to give ease and delight, but it is that very unreality which in our more vigorous moments is apt to make him less stimulating than Shakespeare with his uncompromising truth. The fact would seem to be that with the writers to whom the narrative scheme is a matter of first importance there is the tendency always to accept a spiritual convention which is not sincerely their own creation at all, but one which it is easy to apprehend and difficult to dispute, and we, when our own spirit is not quite at concert pitch, are not only willing to do our part of the acceptance, but even grateful for the lowering of tension. But because this often happens in narrative it does not follow that it is necessary to the form, and Mr. Masefield is with Chaucer and Morris in reminding us of this. He, too, has splendidly the gift of telling a story; that the most prejudiced of his critics could hardly dispute. His gifts as a dramatist are unquestionable, but in the technique of drama he has always been apt to fail his creations in some apparently trivial but really vital movement. In his narrative poems he makes no such mistakes.

Mr. Masefield's manner is now perfectly assured. This is not to say that he is quite at all

moments master of his style, but rather that the
work which he is now doing could not conceivably
be mistaken for that of anybody else. That he
writes extremely well is not the whole point, though
the ease to which he has come after long and patient
discipline is in itself a much more admirable thing
than may commonly be realized, and Mr. Masefield is curiously careless in the opportunities
which he gives to detraction. It may be that he is
indifferent, but if so it is an indifference which a
poet does well to avoid. No preoccupation with
the movement of his work can excuse Mr. Masefield, or any writer, for saying of his hero, at a
moment which not only is intended to be but
actually is charged with feeling, that

'As he left the room for the Saddling Paddock
He looked as white as the flesh of haddock,'

which is not alone in its ineptitude. These lapses in
a writer of the first distinction are, however, Mr.
Masefield's peculiar prerogative, and at this time
of day his readers must make up their minds to
accept them as part of the contract, and that once
done they do not really amount to very much when
the reckoning is made. In his narrative poems,
especially, it might be that something of his rare
impetuousness would be lost to Mr. Masefield if
his mood in writing were one of more exact perfection. And although that is obviously a very

dangerous admission to make, it would seem to be
fully justified in this case by the experience of what
is now a long sequence of remarkable achievements
in narrative poetry. Allowing for all blemishes, the
manner here is the manner of mastery, and through
five centuries the masters have shown that with all
their faults they know better than they can be
taught.

In so far as 'Reynard' is a narrative, its hero is
the fox. The fine body of folk who come to the
meet are used admirably by the poet for the purpose of setting before us one deftly outlined character after another — character here always of
comedy strain — but beyond a formal connection
here and there with the main scheme of the poem
they might have been used much to the same end
and in much the same way as a crowd in a country
market-place or, say, a village church congrega-
tion. This is no defect; the Ghost Heath Run is as
fair a device as another for assembling the poet's
figures — as fair as the Canterbury Pilgrimage.
Mr. Masefield justifies his method by giving us an
exhilarating group of men and women, all rich in
quality, and compounded of type and personality
in the way which the best comic art always con-
trives. But apart from this scheme in the poem,
which might have been as well served by making
the chronicle begin and end with the meet as by
carrying it through the long run by Ghost Heath,

there is a further strain of pure narrative effect, and this concerns itself wholly with the mortal struggle and final escape of the small red animal that gives the poem its name. The story is conducted with great spirit and variety, and is a notable addition to the rare successes in animal poetry. Reynard takes his country with fine dramatic effect, and he becomes very much an object of our concern as we read. He is not sentimentalized by the poet, and in his own vagabond kind he crawls at last into his earth, exhausted but safe, a not unworthy fellow of Mr. Ralph Hodgson's Bull. And as he crosses woods and pasture and rivers, Mr. Masefield finds again an opportunity of drawing the English landscape that he loves so well and sees so vividly. There is no contemporary poetry that has in it more deeply the poignancy of the earth than Mr. Masefield's, and in this poem he, perhaps, excels his own tenderness. We think little or nothing of the crowded folk behind as the fox makes his lonely yet perilous way, with death but at a field's distance, across one of those midland counties that have their own very special and intimate beauty. It is, perhaps, an unconsidered effect in Mr. Masefield's poem that while our interest in the hunting's end never fails, the fox yet seems to be a creature apart from the excited pursuit, moving through a world of natural loveliness that is wholly undisturbed by the little tumult of the scarlet-coated field. Ghost Heath cares nothing for the run. But, unconsidered as it may be, the effect is none the less one of very subtle art, being also the one reminiscence in the poem of Mr. Masefield's rare tragic gift.

The story of 'Right Royal,' the horse who wins the Chasers' Cup, is unerring in its construction from start to finish. It is in every way a worthy companion to 'Reynard,' and will be read with sheer imaginative delight by thousands of people who ordinarily are not much concerned with poetry at all. But, over and above this, the poem is a poem. Surrounding the story is a spiritual life which is the genuine shaping of experience, truly Mr. Masefield's own experience, and that, it might almost be said that only, is what poetry must be. Here we have to surrender to the poet and accept his experience, in this case the radical English fervour for sport, as being significant, but we are not asked to enter into a conspiracy with the poet to accept an experience which is not his but merely one of convenience. To find work of which this can be said, and of which at the same time we know that all sorts and conditions of men will share in the delight, is a matter for uncommon gratitude. In doing it no poet of Mr. Masefield's generation is serving his art more truly.

Although it may be said that 'Reynard the Fox' and 'Right Royal' have not in the detail of their workmanship quite uniformly that cameo-like sharpness that is the surest guarantee of permanence in a long poem as it is in a lyric (in all literary forms, in fact, as in Mr. Hardy's novels, for example), there is a general distinction in the work that can only be attained by an excellence in the parts composing the whole. If the texture is not of the very rarest quality, it is always compact and sound, and the cumulative impression is one both of simplicity and of richness. The poems are likely to serve Mr. Masefield's reputation well. The history of this reputation is not an uncommon one, and affords an interesting comment upon public opinion. Fifteen years ago Mr. Masefield's poems caught the ear of a few careful listeners only. It was then a mark of alert culture (following the careful listeners) to praise him. The poet's audience suddenly became a large one with the widening of his own poetic interests and the introduction into his work of certain popular (but by no means worthless) as apart from purely poetic qualities. There was general applause, and alert culture became shy at first, then a little angry, and finally in disdain left Mr. Masefield for the discovery of Mr. S—— and Mr. S——, who in a day or two will likewise be disowned. Alert culture, the truth is, is but the assertive voice from year to year of the very latest literary *débutant;* we have, I suppose, all been there ourselves.

Mr. Masefield has happily been untouched by the coldness of this disapproval, being more concerned in his work, and consoling himself doubtless with the affection of thousands of readers who are simple enough to think that Tennyson and Wordsworth and Milton were great poets. And his poetry has moved in steady and admirable development, until now in his maturity the wheel is coming full circle. Already alert culture is praising him again, just as it has been announcing to an obtuse world the discovery of that new lyric poet, Mr. Thomas Hardy. You are apt to look a little foolish if you continue in disparagement of a man who can write poems like 'Reynard the Fox.' So that until the next turn of chance Mr. Masefield is secure of his greater and his lesser public. And he possesses himself surely enough to make his more durable fame, when chance shall have played all her tricks, a matter of but little doubt.

RUPERT BROOKE

I

POSTERITY, untroubled by the regrets and intimate sorrows of friendship, untouched by the resentment with which we cannot but meet what for a moment seems mere brutality of accident, will see in Rupert Brooke's life, achievement, and death, one of those rare perfections that attain greatness by their very symmetry and fortunate grace. It is truly as though the gods would have this man great; as though, having given him all bright and clear qualities of brain and heart, they were impatient of any slow moving to the authority for which he was marked, and must, rather in divine caprice than in nature, bring him to untimely and bewildering fulfilment. His brief life, with its inevitable intervals of temperamental unrest, was happy in disposition and in event. It shone with many gifts other than the great gift of poetry. Wit, the cleanest kind of chivalry, inflexible sincerity, and the dear courtesy that only the sincere man knows, courage and reverence duly met, intellectual ease and great personal charm and beauty — all these made his friendship one of the most treasurable things of his time. But they did not touch his life to greatness. Had these been the whole story, there would have been nothing to mark his life from many millions that have gone through the world, eager, beautiful, forgotten. His achievement as a poet, definite, memorable, exhilarating, yet reaches its fullness in a volume of work circumscribed enough if we set it beside that by which any other poet establishes his claim to greatness. Finally his death, noble as it was, was yet but one of lamentable multitudes, marking heroism if you will, but not greatness. For it is not lightly that we call men great; it is only once in a while that we single one from the many who do splendidly and fully all that they might do, and say that he among them all is great. But with this man fortune was to be lavish against all example. Although neither his brilliance in life nor his courage in death could place him among the few at whose names the blood of generations thrills, and although his work, sure as it is of durable fame, does not place him with those poets, perhaps a score in the language, who, by the scope and volume of their poetry alone, assert their greatness, yet Rupert Brooke will be a name as surely marked of greatness as any in England. Only once before in our history, I think, has a man passed to so large and just a renown with so unconsidered and slender a warrant. Until April 23d in this year,[1] when this

[1] 1915.

greatly loved boy died at the Dardanelles, Philip Sidney had not found his fellow.

To those of us who see in poetry the perfect flowering of life, the story of Rupert Brooke will always mean chiefly the score or so of poems in which he reached to the full maturity of his genius and gave imperishable expression to the very heart of his personality. Nor will any profound response to his poetry be enhanced by the accident that brought sublimity to his death, either in those who knew and loved him or in these few who from age to age shall build his best renown. Rupert Brooke, as all poets, would wish to stand or fall chiefly by his poetry, and in the ultimate judgment of poetry no external circumstance whatever has the weight of a single word. Not even the fact that the man who wrote the sonnets, than which after long generations nothing shall make the year 1914 more memorable, served and died for England at war, can add one beat to their pulse. The poetry that shines and falls across them in one perfect and complete wave is, as poetry must always be, independent of all factual experience, and comes wholly from the deeper experience of the imagination. To say that only under the actual conditions could these sonnets have been written is not to the point. Experience of the conditions is common enough; the rare thing is the genius of the poet, and we know that this will fulfil itself be the conditions what they may. It is well to be clear in this matter. We must not suppose, as has sometimes been loosely suggested, that Brooke, in answering a national call, was stirred to a new and profounder poetic expression. At the time when his poetic power was moving in its fullness, it happened to find itself concerned with a great national crisis. The intensity with which this crisis seized his imagination produced poetry which must endure; also it determined him to take up arms. But the two results were not dependent on each other, and to pretend that they were is a sophism of the kind that he would scornfully have repudiated. Had he for any reason been disqualified for service, the poetry would have come in no less certain measure. It is intensity of perception that creates poetry.

Rupert Brooke's best poems are secure of the admiration of all who have the wit to praise justly in these things, and it is this renown that he would most have desired. But we must remember that the people who care deeply and with understanding for rare and lovely art are very few; a few thousands, perhaps, out of the many millions of an age. It is only the ineffectual visionary who supposes that the masses of the people will respond directly to the appeal of excellence in poetry or painting, or even in the more popular arts, as music and the drama. The evidence in the matter is plain enough; I do not even know that the fact is lamentable: it is a fact. But there are already, as I believe there always will be, great numbers of people to whom the name of Rupert Brooke means something, while his poetry, strictly speaking, means nothing. There are times when such a thing is unhappy. The interest with which people who are incurably lazy in their higher perceptions will regard a poet who is a navvy, or has no arms, or is mentioned by a bishop, is merely vulgar. But sometimes a poet becomes celebrated among this wider public in a way that makes for good. The homage that has instinctively been paid for three hundred years to Philip Sidney by people who know not a line of his poetry, and scarcely an event of his life, is wholesome and springs from the better parts of human nature. And so it is with Rupert Brooke. His truest fame will be with those who love his poetry, but the many spirits that will quicken at his name, knowing but vaguely of a brief and fortunate life, a brilliant personality, a poetic genius which they will not be curious to explore, a supreme sacrifice, will quicken worthily and to their own good. Always there will be the false gods of popular favour, the charlatans, the panders, the crafty and unscrupulous flatterers of mob-sentimentality, who betray their consciences daily for a little unsavoury power. The people exalt without understanding them, blindly praising, as it were, their own baser instincts. But, blindly too perhaps, the people will also desire and from time to time discover some external symbol of the nobility that is in them also, patiently keeping the balance of the world. Such a symbol, clear, almost spare, yet magnificently complete, is the radiant, perfectly poised story of Rupert Brooke.

II

THE development of Rupert Brooke's poetic power was, it seems to me, unlike that of most poets. The early verse of men who afterwards prove their authenticity generally shows a great emotional force with little intellectual power of arrangement, and a weakly imitative craftsmanship. The emotion will commonly be concerned, partly by personality and partly by acceptance from tradition, with what we may roughly call the more generous normal instincts of mankind, as a delight in the natural world, the lover's worship, hatred of tyranny, the mere high spirits of young and happy limbs, sorrow for the passing of beauty. Of such things is the material of most fine poetry, as it is of nearly all futile versifying, and so it is that early work frequently tells us nothing of its writer's future. We know that the material is there, but there is nothing to show whether or no there will ever be the art to shape it. But in Rupert Brooke's beginnings there is none of this. The volume of 'Poems' published in 1911, which contains work written as early as 1905, when he was eighteen, shows an art curiously personal, skilful, deliberate. It shows, too, an intellectual deftness altogether unexpected in so young a poet, and it shows finally, not always but often, an indifference to the normal material upon which poets good and bad are apt to work from the outset, and in the shaping of which ultimately comes all poetry that is memorable. Nearly every page is interesting on account of its art and intellectual deftness, qualities that we should not expect to be marked. But there are many pages where we do not get the real glow of poetry, and this because the content, it seems to me, often fails to satisfy the demands of poetry. It is true enough to say that it does not matter what subject the poet may contemplate, but there is an implied provision that the subject shall be one that grips his emotions, one, that is to say, that he perceives poetically. It so happens that this capacity in subject-matter for stirring the emotion to poetic intensity is nearly always coincident with a sympathy with the common experience of the world. A poet may write in praise of his mistress as freshly to-day as if none had written before him, but, although we say that he may choose what theme he will, we could not respond to him if he told us in his song that, while he loved his lady and her beauty and his wooing was in all ways prosperous, the thing that he most desired was never to

see her again. We should at once know that the
attitude was a piece of cold intellectuality, that it
was against poetry in substance.

In Rupert Brooke's earliest work there is a strain
of this intellectual coldness. It is difficult, indeed
impossible, to say exactly what was its source. It
may partly have been an immature enthusiasm for
Donne's poetry, partly a concession to University
preciosity, partly a natural instinct that was not
yet coloured by humanity and experience. To
control sentiment was a determination that never
left him, but to control sentiment is not at all the
same thing as being afraid of it, and at the beginning he was apt to be afraid. And he would often
substitute for the natural emotions which most
young poets experience and cannot shape, an intellectual fancy that he cannot have felt with
passion, and shape it with astonishing skill and
attractiveness. Poetry cannot prosper on these
terms; it must sit at the world's fire, or perish.
The most common note that we find in his first
book in illustration of my meaning is the presence
at love's moment of the knowledge that women
grow old and beauty fades. The reflection is true
in fact, but it is not poetically true, and so, in its
present shape, it is false. That is to say, we know
that, although women do grow old, the lover in the
delight of his mistress does not realize this, and
that the assertion that he does is not emotional

passion of conviction but intellectual deliberation. Rupert Brooke goes one step further into danger; not only does he assert that the lover feels something that we know he does not feel, but — it is perhaps an equitable penalty for the first false step — he makes the realization of a fact that we know is not realized in the circumstances, a source of revulsion, when we know that if the lover felt at all about his mistress's old age it would certainly be with peace and surety. It is only a detached intellectual attitude towards a thing fully perceptible to passion alone, that can suffer the illusion that the lover's mood is subject to these external facts. To argue that a woman does really grow old and lose her younger beauty, and so may forgo something of her power, is beside the point; the lover does not hear you, and it is the lover's consciousness alone of which we are speaking. In poetic truth which is the strictest truth, the woman, living in the young man's mood, is adorable beyond change, and if the young man says, 'I worship you, but I know that you will grow old and fade, and that then I shall hate you,' we know that he is speaking not from his heart but from a nimble brain.

We find, then, in a great many pages of this first book, an instrument that on so young lips is efficient and enchanting against almost all example, yet playing a tune that does not come wholly from the heart. Never, I think, has technique reached so great a perfection without corresponding authenticity of impulse. Only half a dozen times in the book do we get such phrases as 'rife with magic and movement,' or 'whirling, blinding moil,' and even in the poems where most we feel the lack of emotional truth, there is a beauty of words that made the book full of the most exciting promise. Already, too, there was in certain poems assurance against the danger that this intellectual constraint might degenerate into virtuosity. In the song beginning

'Oh! Love!' they said, 'is King of kings,'

the intellectual mood, even in the love traffic in which it has been most shy, is adjusting itself finely to the clear and common impulses of mankind, while in 'Dust,' 'The Fish,' 'The Hill,' 'The Jolly Company,' 'Ambarvalia,' 'Dining-Room Tea,' and the lovely opening sonnet,

'Oh! Death will find me, long before I tire
Of watching you . . .'

there is a movement, a perfect visualization of image and a clarity of individual thought, that mark him as being of the great tradition, and endowed with the spontaneity that fellowship in that tradition implies.

In the volume published after his death, Rupert Brooke seems to me to have passed into full and rich communion with the great normal life of the world. There are three poems, 'All suddenly the wind comes soft,' 'The way that lovers use is this,' and 'Mary and Gabriel,' that are just a little formal perhaps, by no means valueless, but touched with some literary memory at a moment when the poetic faculty was not as alert as usual. There are two poems, 'There's Wisdom in Women,' and 'Love,' where the old detached and ironic mood that was once unreal returns not quite happily, and another, 'The Chilterns,' in which it has been transmuted into a gracious and acceptable humour. Also there is a sonnet, 'Unfortunate,' in which there is a reminiscence of the old mood, but it is now treated very reverently and with superb psychological insight. For the rest we have thrilling and adventurous beauty from beginning to end. There is no more tender landscape in English poetry than 'Grantchester,' suffused as it is with a mood that never changes and yet passes between the wittiest laughter and the profoundest emotion with perfect naturalness. The subject-matter throughout the book no longer forces us to dissent or question. It has become wholly merged in the corporate art, and we accept it unhesitatingly as we accept the content of all splendid work. As in all really fine achievement in poetry, there is in his choice of form a glad acceptance and development of the traditions that have been slowly evolved through generations, and a perfect subjection of those forms to his own personality, until a sonnet becomes as definitely his own as if he had invented the external structure. We find, too, that the early constraint, even though it led to a touch of falsity at the time, has not been without its uses. The common emotions of the world he has, after jealous waiting, truly discovered and won for himself, unstaled of the world's usage. His passion is extraordinarily clean, burning among all simple things, clear, untroubled, ecstatic. Except in the two or three pages of which I have spoken, we find everywhere an almost fierce renunciation of anything that would not stir the plain knitters in the sun, with an unwearying determination to translate all this common simple life into the most exact and stirring beauty. It is true that in one or two cases, notably 'Heaven,' the image that he creates of this simplicity of passion is such as not to relate itself easily at first glance to the clear normal thought that is nevertheless its basis if for a moment we consider its significance. When the poet elects to make brief intellectual holiday, so long as he does so in the terms of his own personality, we should do nothing but make holiday gladly with him. And we may well do so at intervals in a book that moves in the high consciousness of rare but natural poetic achievement, alert with the freshness and daring of splendid youth, grave in that profoundest know-

ledge which is imagination; a book that will surely
pass to vigorous immortality.

III

THE first time I saw Rupert Brooke was in the
summer of 1912, a few months after his first volume had been published. The editor of 'Georgian
Poetry,' whose friendship with the poet will itself
make a page in literary history, had invited some of
us to hear about his proposed anthology. There
were then but a few moments in which Brooke and
I could talk together, and all that I can remember
is an impression of an extraordinarily alert intelligence, finely equipped with both wit and pene-
trative power, and resolutely declining to use
either for any superficial effect. I suppose no one of
his years can ever have had in greater measure the
gifts that can be used to make easily swayed admiration gape, or greater temptations so to employ
his qualities: and I am sure that no man has ever
been more wholly indifferent to any such conquests.
Humour he had in abundance, but of witty insincerity no trace. Never was a personality more
finely balanced. It is this that I remember of him
at that first meeting, this that I — and all his
friends — found governing him and bracing his
genius till the end. It has been said that he had
a strain of self-consciousness about his personal

charm and brilliance, that he was a little afraid lest
that side of him should claim too much attention.
To answer the suggestion would be an impertinence. He was properly glad of his qualities; also,
he was properly careless of them. The notion that
any such matter ever occupied his mind for a moment can be nothing but ludicrous to those who
knew him.

After 1912 I saw him several times in London
and in Birmingham. I find a letter shortly after I
had first met him, sending me his book, another in
November speaking of it and some work of my
own, and 'feeling much excited' about the new
repertory work in Birmingham. Nothing more till
March, 1913, when he writes twice, arranging to
come for the night, and asking for precise directions
as to where he shall sit and how be dressed in the
theatre. We stayed up most of the night talking.
In May he sends me a play, and says he is just off to
America for some months. Then, in the summer of
1914, he was back again, and we met in London
after a vehement letter bidding me to a festivity in
any clothes, which is to be immense fun, and if I
haven't a bed he can find me a couch. Also he
means to stay with us again in Birmingham next
week, but he will have been to the dentist and will
not be fit company for human beings. But he came,
and I remember we exhausted the complete theory
of drama in a tea-shop, went to a promenade con-

cert afterwards, and again talked till morning. Also he arranged to take Lascelles Abercrombie, Wilfrid Gibson, and myself in a motor-car to some quiet place where we could discuss 'New Numbers,' which was now being published. A few days later the project is written off as 'I can't get the car that week. My mother demands it on some nefarious political business. We must work out something for later.'

The something for later was never worked out. In the last week of July we lunched twice together in a Soho restaurant. War was threatening. If it broke, he must go; I think it was said in so many words; it certainly was clear. He was still eager about his new fellowship work at Cambridge, but, as one feels now, there was already in the eagerness the note of foreboding, calm indeed and wholly contented, that seemed to touch all his words thereafter till the end. I heard of him from time to time, then came a long and graphic letter after the fall of Antwerp, at which he was present with the Royal Naval Division. 'There was some affair at Antwerp, I remember . . . a burning city, the din of cannonades, a shattered railway-station, my sailors bivouacking in the gardens of a deserted château, refugees coming out of the darkness. . . .' Then, 'not a bad time and place to die, Belgium, 1915.' We met once again. He was on sick leave, and I saw him for an hour in London. He talked of his new sonnets, just written, of Antwerp, of the boredom of training, the great fellowship that comes in fighting. He expected to be in England for some weeks, and it was arranged that I should spend a day or two with him at Blandford. But he went to the Dardanelles almost at once, and on April 23d he died.

FRANCIS LEDWIDGE[1]

FRANCIS LEDWIDGE, coming from Irish peasant stock, for some time living so that his publisher could advertise him as 'The Scavenger Poet,' joined the Royal Inniskilling Fusiliers in 1914, and was killed in Flanders in 1917, at the age of twenty-five, leaving two books of poems, and the material for a third which has since been published.

To these volumes Lord Dunsany has contributed intimate little prefatory notes, full of generous delight in a new poet's work. His preference for individual poems is a matter over which we may differ pleasantly enough; it is no small distinction for any man to have known the shy footfall of genius when it came, and Lord Dunsany has proved his critical sense in the best of all ways. It is with nothing but respect and gratitude for his charming and courageous god-parentage that we question his opinion at a crucial point in his very brief analysis of Ledwidge's poetic quality. He says, in introducing the poet's first book:

I have looked for a poet amongst the Irish peasants because it seemed to me that almost only among them was in daily use a diction worthy of poetry, as well as an

[1] *Songs of the Fields* (1916); *Songs of Peace* (1917); *Last Songs* (1918). Three volumes, with Introductions by Lord Dunsany.

imagination capable of dealing with the great and simple things that are a poet's wares. Their thoughts are in the spring-time, and all their metaphors fresh. . . .

Ledwidge, he concludes, is the poet for whom he has been looking. We believe that underlying this passage is a misconception in general æsthetics, and that the definition arising from it demonstrably fails to fit the particular case of Ledwidge. In its profounder issues poetry depends little enough on the artificial — but not therefore negligible or worthless — culture that a man absorbs from the prosperous condition of his descent and his own early advantages of society and education. In the process, however, by which a poet comes to the final realization of his faculty such things are of considerable moment, and the nature of their influence is not such as is commonly supposed. Every poet, if he is to do work of any consequence at all, has to find himself through tradition; that is an unescapable condition of his function. Native wood-notes wild are no more of the most natural lyrist's untutored sounding than is the bird's ecstasy unaware of the generations, and almost invariably the personal ease of the young poet's song depends upon the degree of intimacy with the poetic resources of his tongue that he has acquired unconsciously by natural inheritance and early association. The most mannered early verse, after the merely imitative period, is nearly always the

work of poets with no assimilated knowledge of
literature in their blood who have suddenly become
conscious of examples that others have never
lacked. One cannot help contrasting with Ledwidge the case of poets such as Mr. Robert Graves
and Mr. Siegfried Sassoon, who set out upon their
poetic careers at twenty, having already made in
the progress of boyhood the sound adjustment to
tradition, the necessity of which some of us had to
waste several precious years of early manhood in
laboriously perceiving and meeting. It is they, and
not Ledwidge, who fetch their first proper tunes to
their own easy impulses, assured of a technical
behaviour that they need not strain at. There are,
no doubt, earlier poems by Ledwidge than any that
Lord Dunsany has published, but we may take it
that in 'Songs of the Fields' we have the first work
of any personal character. And from this through
the three volumes nothing is more notable in the
poet's external habit than his certain progress from
a manner heavy with self-conscious discovery of
English poetry, through which his genius struggles
often but brokenly to its own gesture, to clear
deliverance from this tardy constraint, when he
writes of his own simple and lovely world with no
touch of untutored circumstance, but in the sweet-
est and most delicate tradition of English song.

Whether these poems are printed in chronological
order we are not told, though the dates given in the

last volume suggest that they are, and they are certainly so arranged as to show direct continuity of development. From the beginning there are signs of imaginative waywardness and of the suddenness of inspired thought that are unmistakable in their meaning On the first page we find, 'And the sweet blackbird in the rainbow sings'; and the presence of poetry is clear. But for long the smallest flight is marred by the mannered or insincere turn. The wind 'like a swan dies singing,' the dusk is velvet, the moon is a pilgrim, the harebells ring. Not yet, either, can he use such a word as 'sublime' in 'Ah! then the poet's dreams are most sublime,' with any of the sureness that belongs to mastery. In his anxiety to do well by the demands of poetry for significant figures, moreover, he falls at first often into triviality and sometimes into real gaucherie. The 'woodbine *lassoing* the thorn' is as unimpressive as the crane watching the troutlets' circles grow 'as a smoker does his rings,' and there is the same kind of poverty in 'Autumn's crayon.' Worse than these, as indicating some deeper defect of judgment, from which, however, he wholly recovered, are such phrases as 'fog of blossom,' and 'facefuls of your smiles.' Another uncertainty in his earliest work comes from the occasional confusion — by no means unknown in poets of far greater experience and power — of scientific knowledge with vision. It would be interesting to know something of Ledwidge's adventures in learning; one imagines that his eager mind, something after boyhood, went through a phase of delight in mere contact with formal instruction, and that for a little while to know a fact was as exciting as to realize a thing. Out of such a mood surely comes the little town's '*octagon* spire toned smoothly down,' which is strangely what poetry is not; and yet he could turn his learning sometimes in his verse to right account, as in, 'When will was all the Delphi I would heed.'

These are indications in particular of the general directions in which the first book is weak. Against them, even among the poems that fail in any complete effect, are to be set many tender and exact felicities, such as:

> 'And like an apron full of jewels
>   The dewy cobweb swings . . .'

Or again:

> 'And in dark furrows of the night there tills
>   A jewelled plough . . .'

Or, speaking of a poet,

> 'And round his verse the hungry lapwing grieves.'

Professor de Selincourt recently reminded us of the wonder of two simple words in Milton's

> 'Which cost Ceres *all that* pain . . .'

There is a kindred beauty in this young Irishman's

'Then when the summer evenings fall serene,
Unto the country dance his songs repair,
And you may meet *some* maids with angel mien,
Bright eyes and twilight hair.'

To these may be added

'And when the sunny rain drips from the edge
Of midday wind, *and meadows lean one way* ...'

and the thought of April who

'Will have a cuckoo on her either shoulder ...'

and the slight, surprising, mastery of

'I watch an apple-spray
Beckon across a wall as if it knew
I wait the calling of the orchard maid.'

It is interesting to note that of the half-dozen or so poems in 'Songs of the Fields' that have a legendary or historical source, all but one have little to distinguish them from the exercises of a true poet, while that one is, unexpectedly, the most completely successful poem in the volume. The explanation is, probably, that the set subject-matter at once subdued the natural play of his genius, and, by keeping him intent on an external responsibility, held him from the excesses to which he was yet liable in his freer meditation. And so, when with such a theme his faculty did for once break through restraint and soar above the occasion, as it did in 'The Wife of Llew,' he wrote what seems to me, if the arrangement of the book is significant, to be his first delicate masterpiece:

'They took the violet and the meadow-sweet
To form her pretty face, and for her feet
They built a mound of daisies on a wing,
And for her voice they made a linnet sing
In the wide poppy blowing for her mouth.
And over all they chanted twenty hours.
And Llew came singing from the azure south
And bore away his wife of birds and flowers.'

It is fragile, a thing partly of the fancy; it has not
the vivid and intimate contact with reality that
was to make some of the later songs of such fine
bearing in their little compass, but it is a lovely
device, surely done. There are three other poems
in this first volume that may be chosen for their
rounded achievement as distinct from occasional
excellence: 'The Coming Poet' (though the first
stanza is hardly good enough for the second),
'Evening in February,' and 'Growing Old,' with
its perfect conclusion:

'Across a bed of bells the river flows,
    And roses dawn, but not for us; we want
The new thing ever as the old thing grows
    Spectral and weary on the hills we haunt.
And that is why we feast, and that is why
We're growing odd and old, my heart and I.'

'Songs of the Fields' is a book full of expectancy.
The reader leaves it in the assurance of an impulse
that will overcome all its difficulties, and break
presently from hesitant and alloyed grace into sure
and bright authority. The development came,
beautifully, and, in a few happy moments of com-

plete liberation, to the height of promise, but it was won with tragic difficulty in the preoccupation into which the poet was called, and in which he was finally to perish. 'Songs of Peace,' issued after an interval of a year, and presumably containing work most of which was written in that time, opens with Ledwidge's longest poem, 'A Dream of Artemis.' Here and there are slack lines, as, 'Such music fills me with a joy half pain,' and the poem generally, although it has dignity, and although its 'Hymn to Zeus,' has lovely touches in it, is unimportant in the body of the poet's work. From a word in Lord Dunsany's preface, however, we gather it to be of earlier composition than the rest of the book. The short lyric, 'A Little Boy in the Morning,' has a first verse of lucky gaiety that is hardly maintained in the second. Then follows a series of poems under divisional headings, 'In Barracks,' 'In Camp,' 'At Sea,' 'In Serbia,' and so on, in which for many pages disappointment seems to be the destined end of our hopes. Still we have the frequent witness that here is a poet of the true endowment:

'The skylark in the rosebush of the dawn,'

a beautiful image that he uses twice, by the way or the right sort of particularity in

'Dew water on the grass,
A fox upon the stile . . .'

but still the full and easy realization of the manifest

gift is deferred. The earlier blemishes are seldom present — it is but once and again we come across words of such relaxed imagination as 'filigree,' and yet the positive advance in creation waits. Then, towards the end of the book, we come to a poem headed, 'Thomas McDonagh,' of which Lord Dunsany says, 'Rather than attribute curious sympathies to this brave young Irish soldier, I would ask his readers to consider the irresistible attraction that a lost cause has for almost any Irishman.' The political equation in the matter does not concern us here, nor does it concern anybody in the presence of what happens to be Ledwidge's first encompassing of profound lyric mastery. Its occasion was, certainly enough, an accident; we know that these enfranchisements of the spirit are dependent upon no outward circumstance. Here is the poem:

> 'He shall not hear the bittern cry
>   In the wild sky, where he is lain,
> Nor voices of the sweeter birds
>   Above the wailing of the rain.
>
> 'Nor shall he know when loud March blows
>   Thro' slanting snows her fanfare shrill,
> Blowing to flame the golden cup
>   Of many an upset daffodil.
>
> 'But when the Dark Cow leaves the moor,
>   And pastures poor with greedy weeds,
> Perhaps he'll hear her low at morn
>   Lifting her horn in pleasant meads.'

The first stanza seems to me to be flawless, the second to have one slightly insensitive phrase — 'fanfare shrill' — and an epithet in the last line that, while it is exactly appropriate, is somehow not perfectly used, while in the last stanza the precisely significant 'greedy weeds' falls doubtfully on the ear. For the rest, it is a poem of that limpid austerity that comes only from minds slowly but irresistibly disciplined to truth. Its inspiration is a quality that, while it is immeasurably precious to those who can perceive it, escapes the sense of many altogether. It has mystery, but it is the mystery of clear modulation and simple confidence, not that other mystery of half-whispered reticence and the veiled image; it is at once lucid and subtle, and it has the repose of vision, not of fortunate dream; it is of the noon, not of the dusk. Preferences in these matters are temperamental; there will always be many more to divine the spirit of wonder in the depths and distances of a Corot than in the flat perspicuousness of a Cotman, but for some the very ecstasy of revelation is touched by the Norwich drawing-master. So it is with poetry; the shy song, the shadow-haunted, with its ghostly quavers and little reluctances, makes its own gentle and enchanted appeal, but for some of us it often leaves half-created what in intention was but to be half-said. For us, the power of presenting, in hard and definite outline, experience perfectly adjusted by the imagination to figures of reality, with imagery that never denies its relation to some intellectual concept and design by claiming sufficiency for itself, is the most hardly won and richest gift of poetry. It was to this power that Ledwidge's development moved, in the poem just quoted, where he comes first to its unquestionable exercise. Like all fine verse, it needs to be read not in silence only, but also aloud.

From this point in 'Songs of the Fields' we have two other poems, 'The Wedding Morning' and 'September,' of, perhaps, as rare a quality, and two others, 'Thro' Bogac Ban' and 'The Blackbirds,' of almost equal attainment, and in 'Last Songs' at least half the poems are written with assured lyric maturity and lightness. 'Autumn,' 'Pan,' 'To One Who Comes Now and Then,' and 'Had I a Golden Pound,' are, it may be, the most striking of them. This is the last-named:

'Had I a golden pound to spend,
　My love should mend and sew no more.
And I would buy her a little quern
　Easy to turn on the kitchen floor.

'And for her windows curtains white,
　With birds in flight and flowers in bloom,
To face with pride the road to town,
　And mellow down her sunlit room.

'And with the silver change we'd prove
　The truth of Love to life's own end,
With hearts the years could but embolden,
　Had I a golden pound to spend.'

The book, which, as a whole, is decidedly the poet's best, has little of the war in it, and only once, in the charming 'Soliloquy,' is there a martial note, and there it is sounded in a slightly conventional contrast with a gayer mood. His songs, here as in the beginning, are almost always of the quiet fields of Ireland or the quiet fields of the mind, and his tenderness for this tranquil and fertile world was not, as it has so often and less significantly been, the fruit of reaction against the squalor and confusion of war. He went to France bearing it in his heart, and there it prospered, in witness of his natural vocation, until he was killed.

Such a gift as that of a few lovely lyrics was at no time greatly esteemed by the world, and in these days, although love of beauty is by no means rare, indifference often smoulders into open hostility. And yet the world's esteem is so little a thing, and beauty so durable, asking but a little companionship. Ledwidge's poems gain nothing from that other gift that he so devotedly gave, that we so forlornly receive. That the world should spend a poet so may be the tragic necessity of the time's folly, and the poet himself least of all would make dispute about it. But nothing justifies the world's pitiable pretence that in making the supreme sacrifice the poet exalts and sanctifies his art; nothing is meaner than the appropriation to our own hearts of the glory of the soldier's death — a glory which is his alone. It is ours to keep him in remembrance, to realize, it may be, the courage that was his; but the continual insistence not that his devotion is splendid, but that it is upon us that his devotion may splendidly bestow itself, is contemptible. Ledwidge died heroically: that I can reflect with deep reverence; that he died for me I can remember only in forlorn desolation and silence. But his poetry exults me, while not so his death. And it is well for us to keep our minds fixed on this plain fact, that when he died a poet was not transfigured, but killed, and his poetry not magnified, but blasted in its first flowering. People, says Lord Dunsany in a letter, 'seemed to think that one poet dead more or less didn't much matter.' So many people, indeed, find in a poet's untimely death an emotional excitement, which if they were honest with themselves they would have to confess was far from being wholly unhappy, that is more vivid than anything else that they ever get from poetry at all, and if the untimely death is also a noble one, yet more punctual is this facile compassion for the arts. But to those who know what poetry is, the untimely death of a man like Ledwidge is nothing but calamity. There are indeed poets who, dying young with what seems measureless promise unrealized, we may yet feel to have so far outrun the processes of nature in early achievement that the vital spirit could no longer support the strain. Keats was such a one; the constructional perfection of the 'Odes' alone bears witness to an intellectual disciplining of genius so far beyond the normal reach of what was but boyhood, that nature had to sink exhausted under the pressure, and there was, perhaps, little of unhappy accident in the stroke that was but an inevitable squaring of the account. In other words, I cannot but think, however profitless such surmise may be, that if Keats had lived to mature manhood, the poetry of his first youth would have been of far less grandeur than it is. But nothing of this can be said of Ledwidge. His development was slow, and, while it was certain enough, it moved with no remarkable concentration nor to fierce purposes. He was cultivating his glowing lyrical gift with tranquil deliberation to exquisite ends, and nothing is clearer than that when he died he had but begun to do his work. His future was plainly marked. Already he had come through the distractions of imitation to a style at once delightedly personal and in the deepest and richest traditions of English lyric poetry. It is, perhaps, strange that his Irish nature should have sung its homeland in a manner that is, it seems to me, not Irish at all, but so it is. He was coming, in a few songs had come, to mastery in the succession of Wyatt and Herrick and Marvell and the lyrical Wordsworth and Matthew Arnold, and such later poets as Mr. Davies and Mr. Hodgson. And across his gentle maturing, with no providence of beauty won beyond the common achievement of poets thus young, death came violently, with no healing, against nature. His own September of the year came in his life before spring had well gone:

> 'Still are the meadowlands, and still
>   Ripens the upland corn,
> And over the brown gradual hill
>   The moon has dipped a horn.
>
> 'The voices of the dear unknown,
>   With silent hearts now call,
> My rose of youth is overblown
>   And trembles to the fall.
>
> 'My song forsakes me like the birds
>   That leave the rain and grey,
> I hear the music of the words
>   My lute can never say.'

THE END